The Institute of Biology's
Studies in Biology no. 68

Phytochrome and Plant Growth

Second Edition

Richard E. Kendrick
B.Sc., Ph.D.
Senior Scientific Officer, Agricultural University, Wageningen

Barry Frankland
B.Sc., Ph.D.
Senior Lecturer in Plant Biology,
Queen Mary College, University of London

Edward Arnold

First published 1976
Reprinted with additions 1978
Second edition 1983
by Edward Arnold (Publishers) Limited
41 Bedford Square, London WC1 3DQ

ISBN 0–7131–2870–4

Printed and bound in Great Britain at
The Camelot Press Ltd, Southampton

General Preface to the Series

Because it is no longer possible for one textbook to cover the whole field of biology while remaining sufficiently up to date, the Institute of Biology proposed this series so that teachers and students can learn about significant developments. The enthusiastic acceptance of 'Studies in Biology' shows that the books are providing authoritative views of biological topics.

The features of the series include the attention given to methods, the selected list of books for further reading and, wherever possible, suggestions for practical work.

Readers' comments will be welcomed by the Education Officer of the Institute.

1983

Institute of Biology
20 Queensbury Place
London SW7 2DZ

Preface to the Second Edition

Green plants, and ultimately all forms of life, depend upon the utilization of sunlight, as an energy source in the process called photosynthesis. However, the quantity, quality and duration of light can regulate the growth and development of a plant independently of photosynthesis. These responses of a plant to light are collectively referred to as *photomorphogenesis*.

The discovery and isolation of phytochrome, the red/far-red reversible pigment involved in photomorphogenesis, is one of the most exciting chapters in modern biology. It provides an excellent illustration of the nature of the scientific process and the way in which scientific ideas develop.

From the point of view of the biology student the study of plant photomorphogenesis is not only important as an aspect of plant physiology, plant biochemistry or plant ecology but can be used to illustrate general principles of photobiology and developmental biology.

The information in this book is presented in a compact and concise form which should make it suitable as advanced reading for the sixth form student. It should be sufficiently complete to provide background reading for the undergraduate student taking a course in, say plant physiology. This second edition has been completely revised and extensively rewritten to include the latest develoments in this rapidly growing field and incorporates many new diagrams and illustrations.

We are most grateful for the useful comments and criticisms of the first edition from colleagues and workers in the field of photomorphogenesis.

Wageningen and London, 1983

R.E.K.
B.F.

Contents

1 Introduction

1.1 Light and the regulation of plant growth

Light is the energy source on which plants and ultimately all living things depend. However, in addition to its utilisation in the process of photosynthesis (*energy transduction*), light can play an important regulatory role in plant growth (*signal transduction*). Higher animals perceive their surroundings and respond to them through the interaction of eyes, brain and limbs, the visual pigment of the eye being the primary light detector. Although plants, unlike most animals, are sedentary organisms they can be orientated by growth movements which are directionally related to the light source. Such responses maximise the efficiency of light interception by the leaves. Darwin, in his book *The Power of Movement in Plants* published in 1880, first fully documented the ability of plants to grow towards the light. The receptor pigment involved in the *phototropic* movements has yet to be identified.

In addition to directing such tropic movements light controls developmental processes such as seed germination, seedling development and flowering. A number of questions can be asked about these events in the life of a plant. How is it that a plant flowers at a particular time of year? How is it that a seedling ceases rapid extension growth on penetrating the soil surface and develops leaves for photosynthesis before its limited food reserves have been exhausted? How is it that some seeds do not germinate while buried in the soil but do germinate when exposed at the soil surface by cultivation? The questions can be rephrased to elicit different kinds of answers. What is the environmental stimulus involved? How is the stimulus perceived? What are the processes involved in producing the appropriate response?

In the case of seed germination and seedling development the environmental stimulus is simply the presence of light. Plants have evolved a mechanism for detecting radiant energy, the ability to do so clearly conferring a selective advantage. The regulation of plant growth and development in relation to the light environment is of obvious importance to a sedentary organism dependent on light as its energy source. Responses are not only to the presence or absence of light but also to variation in the quantity and quality of light. For instance, plants growing in a shaded situation tend to be taller and have a greater leaf area to plant weight ratio than those growing in full sunlight. Responses may also be observed at the sub-cellular level. The disc-shaped chloroplasts of many plants become orientated so that their maximum cross-section is towards the light at low light levels allowing maximum light absorption. At very high light levels they become orientated so that their minimum cross-section is towards the light thus protecting the photosynthetic pigments from damage.

Light duration is also an important regulatory factor. For instance, the length of the day is the environmental factor which provides the most accurate indication of the time of year and plants may respond to a change in the length of the day with a dramatic change in their pattern of development. This phenomenon is termed *photoperiodism*. The best known example is the induction of flowering. Other examples are the onset of bud formation and leaf fall in deciduous trees in response to the short days of autumn.

These various *formative* effects of light are collectively referred to as *photomorphogenesis*. Although they have been known for a long time, it was not until 1935 that any advance was made towards the discovery of the receptor pigment involved. Flint and McAlister working with lettuce seeds found that the wavelengths of light most effective in promoting germination were in the red region of the spectrum (see Fig. 1–5). They also showed that germination could be inhibited by light in the far-red region of the spectrum (Fig. 1–1). In

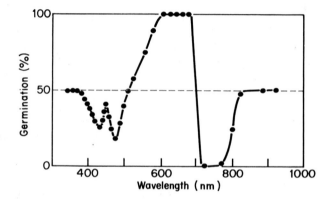

Fig. 1–1   The effect of different wavelengths of light on the germination of lettuce seeds partially induced by red light. Shows that red light (600–700 nm) is most effective in promoting germination and far-red light (700–750 nm) is most effective in inhibiting germination. (Redrawn from Flint, L. H. and McAlister, E. D. (1973. *Smithsonian Inst. Misc. Collections*, **96**, 1.)

1945 a large spectrograph was constructed at the Plant Industry Station of the United States Department of Agriculture, Beltsville, Maryland. This enabled Borthwick and Hendricks, and their co-workers, to determine the relative effectiveness of different wavelengths of light in bringing about particular responses, i.e. action spectra (see § 1.4).

In 1922 Garner and Allard discovered that the length of the day was the critical factor in the control of flowering. They distinguished between short day plants (SDP) which flower when days become shorter than a critical length in late summer and long day plants (LDP) which flower as days grow longer than a critical length in early summer. Later Hamner and co-workers showed that it was the length of the dark period rather than the length of the light period which was measured by the plant. A SDP such as soybean or cocklebur could be prevented from flowering under short days by exposing it to light for a few min in the middle of the night (Fig. 1–2). Clearly the amount of light energy involved here is too small for the effects to be accounted for in terms of difference in photosynthesis. The action spectrum for this response pointed to a receptor pigment with an absorption spectrum (see § 1.3) significantly different from that of chlorophyll, although having a peak in the red region of the spectrum. A similar experiment was carried out with the LDP barley and henbane under short days but in this case a light break given in the middle of the night induces flowering (Fig. 1–2). Action spectra for this response showed a close similarity to those for the inhibition of flowering in SDP.

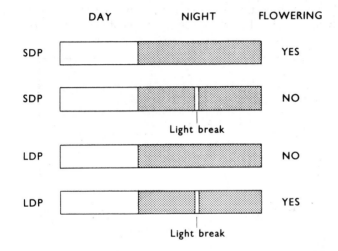

Fig. 1–2 The effects of a light break in the middle of the night on flowering of short day plants (SDP) and long day plants (LDP) when they are grown under short days.

Seedlings which are grown in the dark show characteristic symptoms such as elongated stems and poor leaf development. These symptoms are collectively referred to as *etiolation* and were studied as early as 1754 by Bonnet. Short irradiations with light are sufficient for de-etiolation. Action spectra of such responses (e.g. the promotion of leaf development in pea seedlings) were shown to be very similar to those found in the case of flowering, indicating a common receptor pigment. Responses of albino plants, i.e. plants lacking chlorophyll, proved to be the same as those of normal green plants, confirming the suggestion that the photosynthetic system was not involved.

1.2   Red/far-red reversibility

Detailed action spectra were determined for the promotion of lettuce seed germination and shown to be similar to those determined in flowering and de-etiolation experiments. The wavelength of maximum effectiveness was 660 nm (red light, R). An action spectrum of the inhibition of the lettuce seeds that germinate in darkness showed a peak of effectiveness at wavelength 730 nm (far-red light, F). A most significant observation was that F not only inhibited germination but could reverse the promoting effect of a previous irradiation with R (Fig. 1–3). The reversal by F of the effect of R can be repeated many times, the germination response depending on the final wavelength of light given. It was concluded that the promotion and inhibition of germination by R and F were mediated by a single pigment.

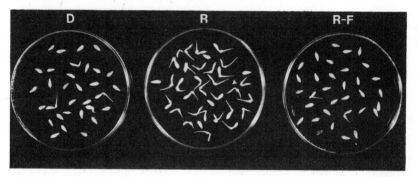

Fig. 1–3   Red/far-red reversibility in light stimulated germination of lettuce seeds. D, dark; R, received 3 min red light; R–F, received 3 min red light followed by 3 min far-red light.

Since the action spectrum for promotion of germination coincided with those for flowering and seedling photomorphogenesis attempts were made to see if F could also reverse the effects of R in these cases. Eventually R–F reversibility was demonstrated for flowering and many de-etiolation phenomena. Typical action spectra for the opposing effects of R and F are shown in Fig. 1–4. In 1952 Borthwick and Hendricks proposed that a R–F reversible pigment existed in the plant which had an inactive R–absorbing form (called Pr) and an active F–absorbing form (called Pfr).

$$Pr \underset{\text{far-red}}{\overset{\text{red}}{\rightleftharpoons}} Pfr$$

Action spectra were taken as an indication of the absorption spectrum of the pigment, suggesting that it was blue-green in colour.

1.3   Absorption spectra

Light is a form of electromagnetic radiation. In common with other electromagnetic radiations it travels at a velocity $c = 3 \times 10^8 \text{ms}^{-1}$. The electromagnetic spectrum, ranging from very short wavelength (λ) cosmic rays

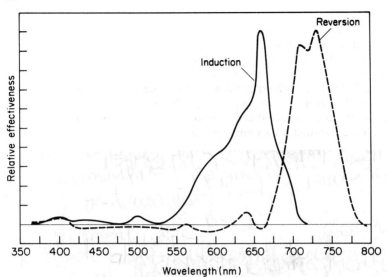

Fig. 1–4 Typical action spectra for red/far-red reversible photoresponses. The spectra are for the induction and reversion of plumular hook opening of etiolated bean seedlings. They are very similar to action spectra of other red/far-red reversible responses, such as promotion of lettuce seed germination. (Redrawn from Withrow, R. B., Klein, W. H. and Elstad, V. (1957). *Plant Physiol.* **32**, 453.)

$(\lambda < 10^{-12}m)$ to long wavelength to radio waves $(\lambda < 10^{-1}m)$ is shown in Fig. 1–5. Visible light is that portion of the spectrum that can be detected by the human eye, i.e. of wavelength between 380 and 750 nm (1 nm = 10^{-9}m). Visible light is bounded by the near ultra-violet on the short wavelength side and the near infra-red on the long wavelength side. Most organic compounds in a plant absorb ultra-violet light but a few, called pigments, also absorb in the visible region of the spectrum by virtue of their extended π-electron systems.

The quantum theory of radiation transfer as proposed by Planck states that transfer of radiation takes place in discrete packets of energy which he called *quanta*. Mathematically this was written:

$$E = h\nu$$

Where E is the energy of a single quantum, h is Planck's constant and ν is the frequency. Later Einstein extended this theory to light and called the energy of a single quantum of light a *photon*. Since frequency is inversely related to wavelength it follows

$$E = h\frac{c}{\lambda}$$

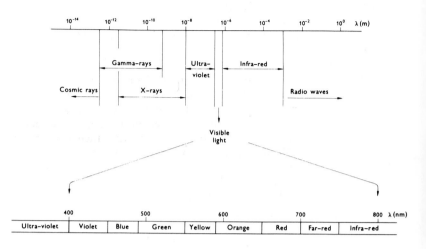

Fig. 1–5   The electromagnetic spectrum.

Photons of short wavelength are more energetic than photons of longer wavelength.

For a single molecule to undergo a photoreaction it must absorb one quantum of energy (hv). Therefore one mole of a compound would absorb N ($N = 6.024 \times 10^{23}$, the Avogadro number) quanta. This amount of light is referred to as a mole of photons. The energy of a mole of red light is less than a mole of blue light, although both have the same number of photons.

Light is usually measured by an instrument, such as a radiometer, whose response is proportional to the radiant energy, rather than the number of photons, falling on the surface of the detector. Therefore, biologists very frequently express light doses in terms of energy per unit area, e.g. J (joules) m^{-2}. Light intensity, or what is more properly called *irradiance* or *energy fluence rate* or *radiant energy flux*, is expressed as energy per unit area per unit time, i.e. J m^{-2} s^{-1}, or power per unit area i.e. W (watts) m^{-2}. The illumination of a surface by white light is often measured by a photometer in units of lux (lumens m^{-2}). Such units of illuminance cannot be converted directly into irradiance units and can only be used for comparing light sources of a similar spectral quality. 1 lux at 555 nm is equivalent to 1.61 mW m^{-2}. The quantum equivalent of irradiance is called *quantum flux density* or *photon fluence rate* and is expressed in units of mol m^{-2} s^{-1}. The product of photon fluence rate and irradiation time gives the quantum dose or *fluence* (mol m^{-2}). 1 J m^{-2} at 600 nm is equivalent to 5 μmol m^{-2}.

When a molecule absorbs a quantum of light its energy is increased. This is represented by the excitation of an electron to a higher energy level. Two electrons cannot absorb one photon nor can one photon excite two electrons. When an electron absorbs a photon it is said to be in an excited state as opposed

to the ground state. For individual atoms the absorption of a single quantum of
energy can be followed by a sharp line in its absorption spectrum at the
wavelength λ given by $\Delta E = hc/\lambda$. In a molecule consisting of different atoms
the transitions from ground to the excited state can take place by absorption of
light quanta of varying amounts of energy, the sharp line in the absorption
spectrum being replaced by a broader absorption band. An excited state can
revert to the stable ground state with the emission of a quantum of light.
Whereas with an atom the absorption and emission takes place at the same
wavelength, in a molecule the peak of the emission (e.g. fluorescence)
spectrum is at a longer wavelength (i.e. lower energy) than that of the
absorption spectrum. The absorption spectrum is characteristic of a molecule
and it gives an indication of the nature of its chemical structure. Coloured
organic compounds, i.e. those that absorb visible light, have highly conjugated
systems of π-electrons. An example is the porphyrin ring of chlorophylls.

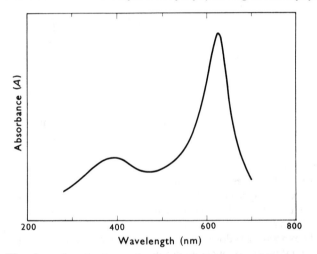

Fig. 1–6   The absorption spectrum of a hypothetical pigment. Absorbance plotted
against wavelength.

The absorption spectrum (Fig. 1–6) can be defined as a graph of absorbance
(A) of a pigment plotted against wavelength (λ). The absorbance of a pigment
is measured by a spectrophotometer. This instrument provides monochromatic light of various wavelengths at which the absorbance can be
measured. This has to be carried out under certain standard conditions (Fig.
1–7). Pigment solution is placed in a cuvette through which the light is passed.
Correction has to be made for light reflected at the surface of the cuvette and
light absorbed by the solvent. This is done by comparing with an identical
cuvette holding the same solvent but lacking the pigment under investigation
(called the blank or reference cuvette). The light flux emerging from the
cuvette is measured by means of a photosensitive device such as a
photomultiplier tube.

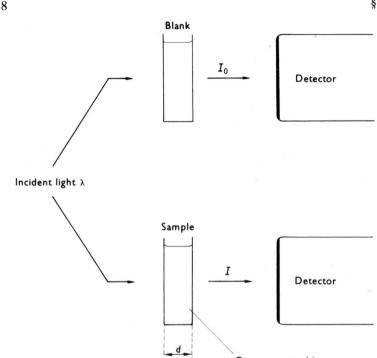

Fig. 1-7 The principle of absorbance measurement using a spectrophotometer. Arrows indicate the direction of the monochromatic light beam. I_0, is the light flux transmitted by the reference or blank cuvette; I, is the light flux transmitted by the sample cuvette; d, is path length and c, the pigment concentration.

Beer's law states that the absorbance (A) is proportional to the concentration (c) of the pigment:

$$A = \log_{10}\frac{I_0}{I} \propto c \text{ (if the path length } d \text{ is constant)}$$

where I_0 is the light flux from the blank cuvette and I is the light flux from the sample cuvette.
Also:

$$A \propto d \text{ (if the concentration } c \text{ is constant)}$$

Therefore:

$$A = \epsilon\, cd$$

where ϵ is the combined proportionality constant and is called the *molar extinction coefficient* (mol dm³ cm⁻¹) i.e. the A of a 1 molar solution of 1 cm pathlength. On a weight basis (g dm³ cm⁻¹) the constant is the *absorption coefficient* (α). ϵ plotted against wavelength gives the absorption spectrum of the pigment. The absorption spectrum of a pigment is characteristic of the pigment and indicative of a particular chemical structure.

1.4   Action spectra

An action spectrum is a graph of the effectiveness of different wavelengths of light in bringing about a particular biological response. As seen in section 1.3 a response initiated by a photoreaction requires the absorption of discrete quanta. The first step in determining an action spectrum is to determine the number of quanta of different wavelengths required to bring about the response. This involves plotting fluence-response curves for each wavelength. It is necessary to show that there is 'reciprocity' over the range of fluence rates (N) and irradiation times (t) used, that is, response is proportional to fluence (Nt). It is important to plot the response against the fluence, because as pointed out earlier quanta of different wavelength contain different amounts of energy. In photobiological studies where signal transduction (e.g. phytochrome in photomorphogenesis) rather than energy transduction (e.g. chlorophyll in photosynthesis) is involved it is usual to plot fluence on a logarithmic scale. A standard response is chosen (X in Fig. 1–8) and the number of quanta of each wavelength required to bring about this response are measured. The lower the number of quanta of a particular wavelength required the more effective that wavelength is in bringing about the reaction. A plot of $1/Nt$, where Nt=fluence

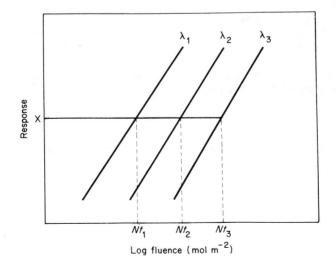

Fig. 1–8   Fluence-response curves enable the fluence (Nt) of different wavelengths of light (λ_1, λ_2, λ_3) required to bring about a standard response (X) to be determined.

to bring about the standard response, against λ (wavelength) is called the action spectrum. It should be the same shape as the absorption spectrum of the receptor pigment (Fig. 1–6), providing screening pigments are not present.

An action spectrum provides a powerful tool in determining the nature of a receptor pigment involved in a biological response. This is especially true when the pigment is very dilute and not easily seen. Since an action spectrum has the same form as the absorption spectrum it gives an indication of the chemical structure of a receptor pigment even before the latter has been physically detected. This arises because response is proportional to the product of number of photons absorbed, Nt, and *quantum yield* or quantum efficiency, Φ.

$$\text{Response} \propto Nt.\epsilon.\Phi$$

Provided Φ does not vary with wavelength then, for the selected standard response, ϵ is proportional to $1/Nt$.

2 Phytochrome Detection and Isolation

2.1 Historical aspects

On the basis of action spectra for red(R)/far-red(F) reversible responses in plants it was predicted that there was a photoreversible pigment existing in two forms, Pr (R-absorbing) and Pfr (F-absorbing), which were respectively blue and green in colour. Action spectra suggested that the absorption spectrum of

$$\text{Pr} \underset{\text{far-red}}{\overset{\text{red}}{\rightleftarrows}} \text{Pfr}$$

the R-absorbing form was similar to the photosynthetic pigment c-phycocyanin of cyanobacteria (blue-green algae). This is known to consist of an open-chain tetrapyrrole chromophore attached to a protein (Fig. 2–1). In 1952 the presence of such a pigment in a plant could only be inferred from the R–F reversible nature of a physiological response. At this time attempts were made to detect phytochrome by physical means. Seedlings grown in the dark and albino maize (*Zea mays*) plants were first examined, since these plants lack chlorophyll which would obviously mask any other green pigment. However, such seedlings are yellow rather than blue or green in colour despite the fact that they exhibit R–F reversible responses. This indicated that the pigment, if present, was in a very low concentration.

Alternating exposure to R and F should induce changes in absorbance in a sample containing the pigment, and a properly designed and sufficiently sensitive spectrophotometer should be able to detect such changes. A sample

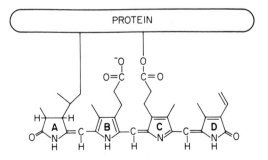

Fig. 2–1 The structure of the open-chain tetrapyrrole chromophore of phytochrome and its mode of attachment to the protein.

consisting of plant tissue is very different from a clear solution (see § 1.3). The samples are optically dense because they exhibit light scatter brought about by variation in refractive index throughout the tissue (see § 2.2). An instrument was already available at Beltsville for work on optically dense material, and in 1959 it was used by Butler and co-workers to look for differences in absorption spectra between R-irradiated and F-irradiated dark-grown maize seedling tissue. Differences were immediately found (Fig. 2–2) with the maximum fall in absorbance being at 730 nm and the maximum rise in absorbance being at 660 nm in going from R-irradiated to F-irradiated tissue. The photo-morphogenetic pigment was now physically detected, and it was at this time that the name *phytochrome* (meaning 'plant pigment') was first proposed by Butler. Within hours of it being detected in tissue by spectrophotometry an aqueous extract was prepared and shown to contain phytochrome. The photoreversible properties were lost on boiling, suggesting that the

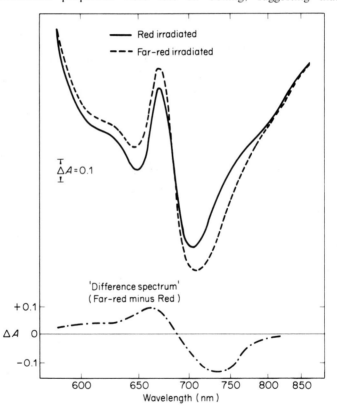

Fig. 2–2   First reported 'difference spectrum' for phytochrome. The upper curves are the actual absorbance after saturating exposures to red and far-red light and the difference is shown below. (Redrawn from Butler, W. L., Norris, K. H., Siegelman, H. W. and Hendricks, S. B. (1959). *Proc. Nat. Acad. Sci. U.S.A.*, **45**, 1703.)

phytochrome chromophore was attached to a protein. In 1964 Siegelman and Firer used this knowledge to develop a method of purification of phytochrome from etiolated seedlings (see § 2.6.).

2.2   Spectrophotometry of optically dense samples

Unlike clear solutions optically dense samples do not obey Beer's Law (see § 1.3). When a sample is placed in a spectrophotometer most of the light falling on the cuvette is lost because of scatter. That light which emerges from the rear of the cuvette does so in all directions. The sensitivity of a spectrophotometer depends on the signal-to-noise ratio, S/N

$$\frac{S}{N} \propto I$$

where I=light flux falling on the detector (photomultiplier). It is therefore important with an optically dense sample to have measuring beams of high intensity and to collect as large a solid angle of the emergent light as possible by placing the detector very close to the sample. When measuring the products of a reversible photoreaction the measuring beams cannot be of too high a flux or they will bring about pigment photoconversion. For a light scattering sample:

apparent absorbance (A)=scatter+real absorbance

real absorbance$=\beta \epsilon c d$

where β=scattering factor; ϵ=extinction coefficient; c=average concentration of pigment; d=path length (sample thickness). The scattering essentially increases the path length by producing a tortuous path along which a quantum of light has greater probability of being absorbed. Other things being equal the presence of scatter gives an amplification of the absorbance by increasing path length. This factor is important and makes detection of low pigment concentrations possible. An assay system which measures in an optically dense system must in some way compensate for that fraction of the light lost due to scatter.

2.3   The spectrophotometric assay

The most widely used assay for phytochrome has been the dual-wavelength method. This involves measuring the apparent absorbance at two wavelengths and subtracting them to give an absorbance difference (ΔA). This difference is a measure of the real absorbance difference at the two wavelengths since the scatter components of the apparent absorbances at the two wavelengths are equal and therefore cancel out. In the case of phytochrome the wavelengths used depend on the material concerned. Initially the beams are set at the peak absorbances of Pr and Pfr, 660 and 730 nm respectively. The ΔA is then measured after sequential irradiations with R and F to bring about phytochrome conversion (Fig. 2–3). Obviously, using these wavelengths changes in ΔA after R will arise from both a loss of Pr and a gain of Pfr. Therefore the magnitude of the ΔA change is approximately twice that corresponding to the amount of phytochrome present. Pr and Pfr can be measured separately if the wavelengths 660 and 730 nm are used independently with a reference wavelength of 800 nm at which phytochrome has little, if any, absorbance.

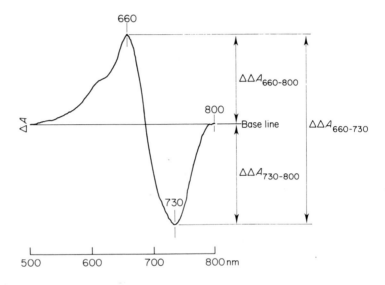

Fig. 2–3 Diagram of the absorbance changes measured in the phytochrome assay. Baseline determined after red light and the 'difference spectrum' obtained by far-red irradiation. See text for details.

The *in vivo* assay cannot be used with tissues that contain more than a small amount of chlorophyll as the measuring light beams are absorbed by chlorophyll as well as by phytochrome. This precludes measurement in green leaves, although phytochrome is detectable in achlorophyllous tissues from plants grown in the light such as white flower petals and white regions of variegated leaves. This means that most of our knowledge of phytochrome *in vivo* comes from studies on etiolated tissues which are rich in phytochrome and low in chlorophyll. However, tissues grown in the dark often contain a little of the precursor of chlorophyll, protochlorophyllide. When irradiated with R this undergoes an irreversible photoreaction to form chlorophyllide, which absorbs at longer wavelengths. At room temperature there is a gradual absorbance shift from longer to shorter wavelength as chlorophyll is formed from chlorophyllide. The light reaction is very rapid and the dark reactions take about 20 min to reach completion at room temperature. At the temperature used for the phytochrome assay (0°C) these dark shifts do not occur. Exposure of tissue grown in the dark to R results in an absorbance increase at 660 nm due to protochlorophyllide conversion and an absorbance decrease at 660 nm due to phytochrome conversion. Often this increase and decrease are about equal. This problem can be partially overcome by giving irradiation with R prior to the R–F–R sequence used to determine the amount of phytochrome in a sample. Chlorophyll artefacts are most noticeable using measuring beam wavelengths of 660 and 730 nm, but can be minimized by using 730 versus 800 nm. In the latter case, of course, the values obtained are about half of those obtained with the 660/730 measuring system (Fig. 2–4).

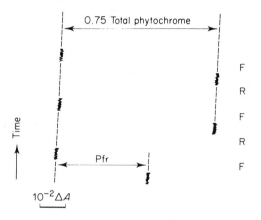

Fig. 2–4 Actual recording of phytochrome measurement in epicotyls of peas. The photoreversible ΔA signal following saturating alternate actinic red (R) and far-red (F) is proportional to 0.75 of the total phytochrome present (see § 2.6). The initial ΔA change after F corresponds to the amount of Pfr in the sample.

One technique used recently to enable detection of phytochrome by spectrophotometry in light-grown plants is the use of the herbicide Norflurazon. Norflurazon inhibits carotenoid biosynthesis and leads to a loss of chlorophyll by photo-oxidation. It does not appear to interfere with the phytochrome system in dark-grown seedlings. Since treated plants lack chlorophyll, and are therefore incapable of photosynthesis, use is usually restricted to young seedlings which are growing at the expense of stored food reserves. Since chlorophyll has a strong screening effect on the phytochrome system, results obtained from measurements of Norflurazon treated light-grown plants need careful interpretation.

  Figure 2–5 shows the principle of operation of a dual-wavelength spectrophotometer. The exact construction varies considerably, but a simple version is shown in Fig. 2–6. This spectrophotometer uses interference filters to obtain the measuring beam wavelenghts λ_1 and λ_2 which are sequentially irradiated on to the sample by means of a rotating sectored mirror. Provision is made for the introduction of a prism and photomultiplier shutter so that the sample can be irradiated with actinic light to photoconvert the phytochrome.

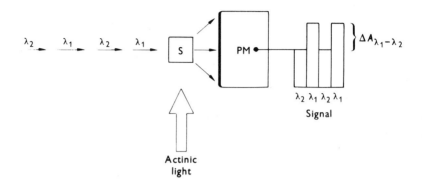

Fig. 2–5   Schematic diagram of a dual-wavelength spectrophotometer. The measuring beams of wavelength λ_1 and λ_2 fall successively on to the sample cuvette (S). The photomultiplier (PM) measures the light of each wavelength emerging from the sample and the corresponding signals are compared to give a direct absorbance difference $\Delta A_{\lambda_1 - \lambda_2}$. Also provision is made for photoconverting the pigment in the sample cuvette with actinic light.

Although the dual-wavelength method is the most sensitive it only enables individual wavelengths to be examined. To obtain a complete 'difference spectrum' for the reaction Pr $\overset{h\nu}{\longrightarrow}$ Pfr it is necessary to make measurements at many wavelengths. A second method is available which enables the whole spectrum to be scanned, but this is less sensitive and requires two samples. This is the double-beam technique. As shown in Fig. 2–7 this method involves measuring the difference in absorbance between the two samples before and after photoconversion of phytochrome in one of them from Pr to Pfr. The instrument gives directly the 'difference spectrum', i.e. the difference between a reference cuvette containing Pr and a sample cuvette containing Pfr. Since in other respects the two samples are equal the difference should reflect only photoconversion of phytochrome.

2.4   The immunological assay

Once purified the phytochrome can be used to produce a specific antibody, providing the basis of an alternative assay. This method, pioneered by Pratt and his co-workers, has the advantage of being more sensitive than spectrophotometry and can be used to locate phytochrome within the cell. Tissues to be investigated can be fixed with formaldehyde to preserve structural features, including phytochrome, in their natural place. The tissue is then dehydrated and sectioned. Alternatively, tissue can be frozen, sectioned and then dehydrated. Pratt uses a double indirect immunochemical method to

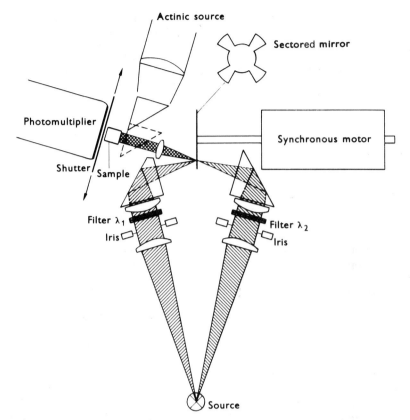

Fig. 2–6 A simple dual-wavelength spectrophotometer. The measuring beams of wavelength λ_1 and λ_2 are obtained by means of interference filters from the same source and they fall successively on the sample by means of a rotating sectored mirror. Iris diaphragms enable the beams to be balanced. Insertion of a prism and closing a protective shutter in front of the photomultiplier enable the sample to be irradiated with actinic light. (Redrawn from Spruit, C. J. P. (1970). *Meded. Landbouwhogeschool Wageningen*, **70**, 1.)

visualize phytochrome (Fig. 2–8). The specific antibody to phytochrome (RAP) is prepared by injecting highly purified phytochrome (P) into a rabbit. The sections to be investigated are rehydrated and incubated with RAP which immunochemically binds to phytochrome in the section (P–RAP). The tissue sections are then treated with sheep anti-rabbit immunoglobulin serum (SAR) which binds immunochemically to the P–RAP complex. An antiperoxidase–peroxidase complex is then immunocytochemically bound to the P–RAP–SAR system. The peroxidase is therefore bound by three specific immunoglobulins to phytochrome. The peroxidase enzyme can then be used to oxidase a

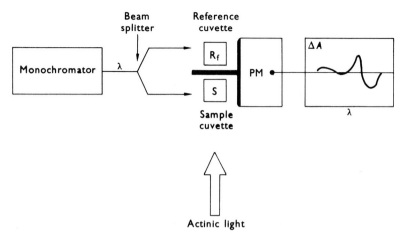

Fig. 2–7 Schematic diagram of a double-beam spectrophotometer. A monochromatic light beam of wavelength λ is split so that it falls successively on to the reference cuvette (R_f) and sample cuvette (S). The light emerging from the two cuvettes is measured by the photomultiplier (PM) and the two signals are adjusted electronically to be equal throughout the spectrum (base line). Only the sample cuvette is then exposed to actinic light and the spectrum scanned to give directly the 'difference spectrum' of the photoreaction.

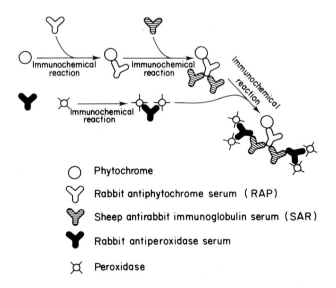

Fig. 2–8 The procedure used for the immunological visualization of phytochrome (see text for details).

substrate (3,3′-diaminobenzidine) in the presence of hydrogen peroxide. The product is bright orange and is insoluble and is retained in the proximity of the enzyme and therefore the phytochrome (Fig. 2–9). Besides the visibility of the product under the light microscope the product is sufficiently electron dense to be visible under the electron microscope (Fig. 2–9). The complexity of the protocol produces an amplification by a factor or a thousand. A technique is now also available in which a fluorescent labelled antibody is substituted for the antiperoxidase–peroxidase complex in Fig. 2–8. Despite its sensitivity, immunocytochemistry has the limitation that it cannot discriminate between Pr and Pfr. However, as well as increased sensitivity it does have the advantage over spectrophotometry in that it can be used to investigate proteolytic degradation products of phytochrome that either lack the chromophore or are not photoreversible.

Recently Hunt and Pratt have developed a radioimmunoassay for phytochrome. This technique allows detection of phytochrome in ng quantities and enables phytochrome to be measured in small-scale crude extracts of light-grown plants (Fig. 2–10). The procedure involves reacting a standard quantity of tritiated (^{3}H) phytochrome with a fixed amount of rabbit antiphytochrome serum (RAP). Using goat antirabbit immunoglobulin serum (GAR) and non-immune rabbit serum (NRS) an immunoprecipitate is formed which can be collected by centrifugation. If a sample for assay containing phytochrome is added to the RAP before the ^{3}H-phytochrome, less radioactivity results in the final pellet. The assay is calibrated by reacting RAP with known quantities of unlabelled phytochrome.

2.5   Distribution and localization

Phytochrome has now been detected in achlorophyllous tissue of many species, particularly in etiolated seedlings. Detailed studies of different parts of seedlings suggest that the highest phytochrome content (about 10^{-6} M) is in the regions of most active growth such as the epicotyl hooks of peas and the coleoptilar node of oats (Fig. 2–11). This type of distribution patter has now been confirmed using immunocytochemistry.

Phytochrome has been detected directly in roots, hypocotyls, cotyledons, coleoptiles, stems, petioles, leaf blades, vegetative buds, floral receptacles, inflorescences and developing fruits and seeds. It has been detected in tissues of both primary and secondary growth. Besides these direct observations indirect evidence from physiological experiments indicates the presence of phytochrome in many other plant materials. Phytochrome has been detected in angiosperms, gymnosperms, pteridophytes, bryophytes and algae. Differences between phytochrome in higher and lower plants are discussed in section 3.5.

2.6   Extraction and purification

The most satisfactory plant material for the extraction of phytochrome has proved to be dark-grown seedlings of monocotyledons such as oats (*Avena*

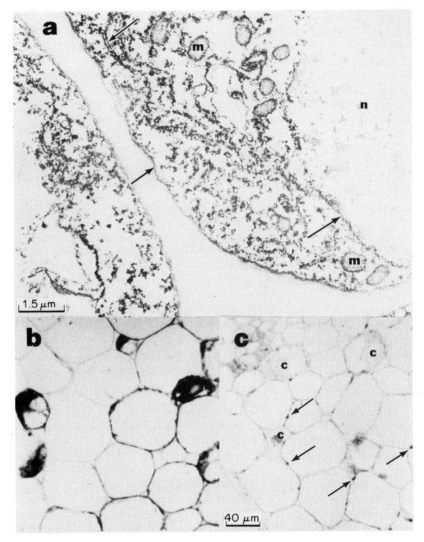

Fig. 2–9 (a) Electron micrograph of oat coleoptile parenchyma cells that have been immunocytochemically stained for phytochrome. Coleoptile tissue fixed prior to light exposure so that phytochrome was present as Pr. Virtually all electron density is associated with phytochrome, n=nucleus, m=mitochondria. Some reaction product appears associated with membranes (arrows). (From Coleman, R. A. and Pratt, L. H. (1974), *J. Histochem. Cytochem*, **22**, 1039. Copyright © by the Histochemical Society, Inc.) **(b)** Light micrograph of oat coleoptile parenchyma cells immunocytochemically stained for phytochrome. Coleoptiles were fixed at 0°C prior to light exposure so that phytochrome was as Pr. These cells have large, central vacuoles, but where extensive

cytoplasm has been sectioned intense uniform stain for phytochrome is visible. **(c)** As in (b) except that the plants received 8 min of red light immediately prior to fixation so that phytochrome, as Pfr is now present as discrete areas (arrows). The general cytoplasm, c, is now unstained. (From MacKenzie Jr., J. M. Coleman, R. A. Brigss, W. R. and Pratt, L. H. (1978). *Proc. Nat. Acad. Sci. U.S.A.*, **72**, 799.)

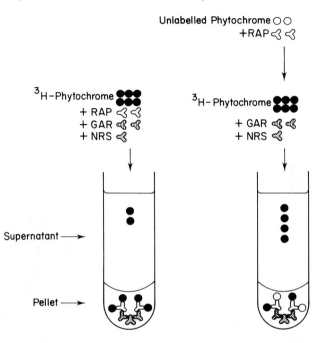

Fig. 2–10 The radioimmunological assay for phytochrome. RAP, rabbit antiphytochrome serum; GAR, goat antirabbit immunoglobulin serum; NRS, non-immune rabbit serum (see text for details).

sativa) and rye (*Secale cereale*). Phytochrome can be extracted from tissues of green plants but only with considerable difficulty.

Phytochrome is readily extracted from oats by grinding dark-grown coleoptile tissue with buffer at a pH higher than 7.3. Below this pH the phytochrome is found in the pellet following centrifugation to remove cell debris. Since phytochrome is only present at low concentration large volumes of tissue and extraction buffer are required. Since it is a protein and therefore labile, especially in crude extracts, low temperatures (0–2°C) are used and a reducing agent such as mercaptoethanol added. The extraction is carried out under a dim green safe-light with the phytochrome in the more stable Pr form.

Figure 2–12 shows the conventional method for the purification of phytochrome. It involves initially grinding the tissue and reducing the large volumes of crude extract to manageable proportions. This is followed by many

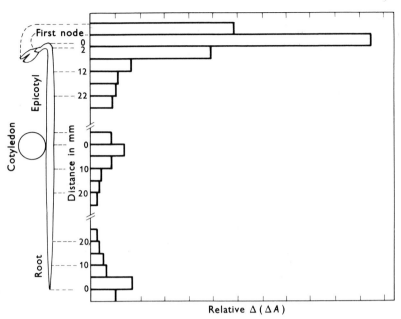

Fig. 2–11 Distribution of phytochrome in an etiolated pea seedling. (Redrawn from Furuya, M. and Hillman, W. S. (1964). *Planta*, **63**, 31.)

purification steps including adsorption chromatography, ammonium sulphate precipitation, gel filtration and ion exchange chromatography to separate phytochrome from the large number of proteins of similar charge and size. Purity or specific activity is assessed by the ratio of absorbance at 660 nm to that at 280 nm (peak of protein absorption) which is 0.8 for pure phytochrome. Purity can be confirmed by electrophoresis on polyacrylamide gels containing sodium dodecyl sulphate (SDS), where pure phytochrome migrates as a single band.

The absorption spectrum of phytochrome in its two forms is shown in Fig. 2–13. The colour was observed to change from blue-green (Pr) after irradiation with F to green (Pfr) after irradiation with R. After action spectra were determined for photoconversion it became clear that R can also photoconvert Pfr to Pr to some extent. This means that a saturating irradiation with R produces a mixture of 75% Pfr and 25% Pr. F produces approximately 3% Pfr and 97% Pr.

The action spectra of physiological responses led Hendricks and his co-workers to speculate that the tetrapyrrole chromophore of phytochrome was similar to that of the photosynthetic pigment c-phycocyanin of cyanobacteria (blue-green algae). The absorption spectrum of purified phytochrome confirmed this view and it was proposed that the chromophore group which gives phytochrome its colour was of the type in Fig. 2–1. The exact nature of

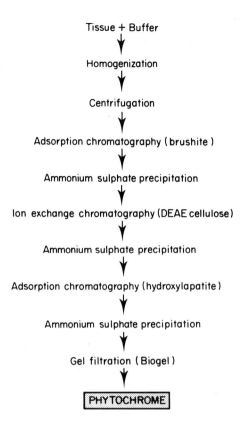

Fig. 2–12 Flow diagram of the conventional procedure for extraction of phytochrome from etiolated oat seedlings.

the chromophore has not yet been determined, mainly because of the difficulty in obtaining the large quantities required for chemical analysis.

Over the years the molecular weight of oat phytochrome became accepted as 60000 daltons in most laboratories. However, Correll using rye as a source obtained a phytochrome preparation of high purity with a higher molecular weight which on storage gave a product with lower molecular weight. Briggs and co-workers in 1972 obtained a partially pure phytochrome preparation from oats with components of 120000 and 60000 molecular weight. After storage for a day in the cold (0–4°C) only the smaller component was found. It was demonstrated that a protease was present in oats which attacked the phytochrome during the early stages of the extraction procedure. This protease degrades the larger molecular weight form of phytochrome to a stable 60000 molecular weight product. Rye contains far less of this endogenous protease and it is therefore simpler to obtain large phytochrome from this source. The nature of the protease was investigated and the extraction procedure was modified to minimize its action.

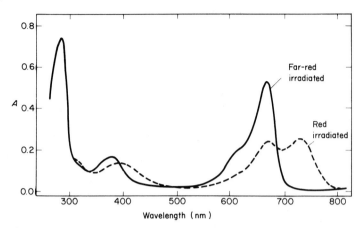

Fig. 2–13 The absorption spectrum of a solution of phytochrome after a saturating exposure to red and far-red light. (Redrawn from Rice, H. V., Briggs, W. R. and Jackson-White, C. J. (1973). *Plant Physiol.*, **51**, 917.)

Two affinity techniques have recently been developed which produce large phytochrome in a much shorter period than the conventional assay. In this way the problem of proteolytic degradation is overcome. One technique involves the use of the specific antibody of phytochrome, and therefore necessitates the intitial purification by conventional means (Fig. 2–14a). However, once operative, the technique is self sustaining. The antibody to phytochrome is immobilized on a column of agarose beads. The crude phytochrome extract is applied to the column and proteins that do not bind specifically are eluted on washing. Phytochrome retained on the column is then eluted with $MgCl_2$ and formic acid. The column is then ready for use in the next extraction.

The second affinity method relies on the fact that phytochrome binds specifically to Cibacron blue immobilized on agarose beads (Cibacron blue-agarose). Once bound to the column phytochrome can be washed free of other proteins and then specifically eluted by flavin mononucleotide (FMN). In the full procedure, adsorption chromatography on brushite is used before the Cibracon blue-agarose column, and there is a final gel filtration step. (Fig. 2–14b). Nevertheless the whole technique can be completed in one day with a very high yield.

Amino acid analyses of 120000 molecular weight phytochrome from zucchini squash (*Cucurbita pepo*), oat (*Avena sativa*) and rye (*Secale cereale*) is shown in Table 1. Phytochrome has an abundance of polar and non-polar amino acids. Immunochemical studies which involve making antisera of large and small phytochrome suggest that when large phytochrome is degraded not only is the 60 000 molecular weight R–F reversible form produced, but also a

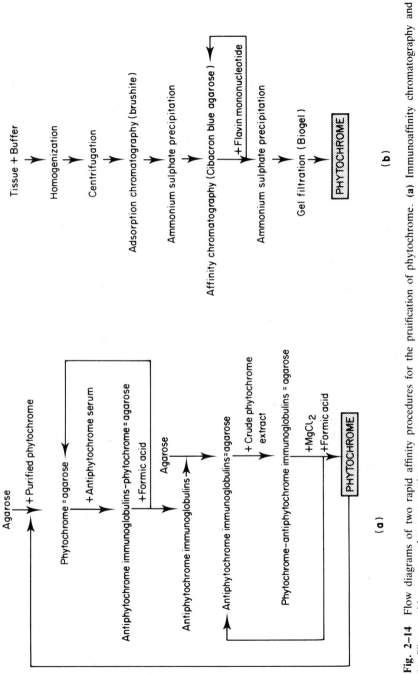

Fig. 2-14 Flow diagrams of two rapid affinity procedures for the pruification of phytochrome. (a) Immunoaffinity chromatography and (b) Cibacron blue-agarose chromatography.

protein that is not photoreversible. It is therefore possible that there is only one chromophore per 120 000 molecular weight form.

There is now evidence that the real native phytochrome has a molecular weight greater than 120 000 and that the difference in absorbance properties between phytochrome studied *in vitro* and that *in vivo* (see Table 2) is associated with the cleaving away of a portion of protein of size about 5000. This cleavage occurs to Pr within a short period of homogenization, while Pfr appears to be protected from attack.

Table 1 Comparison of the amino acid composition of 120 000 molecular weight phytochrome from zucchini squash and oats (Hunt, R. E. (1979) Ph.D. thesis, Vanderbilt University, Nashville, U.S.A.); and rye (Rice, H. V. and Briggs, W. R. (1973) *Plant Physiol.*, **51**, 927). Entries are number of residues to the nearest integer. ND = not determined.

Amino acid	Zucchini	Rye	Oat
lysine	64	55	64
histidine	26	26	34
arginine	50	47	51
aspartic acid	104	97	118
threonine	56	43	38
serine	82	71	73
glutamic acid	126	120	122
proline	58	83	45
glycine	80	73	72
alanine	77	103	93
cystine and cysteine	18	25	27
valine	74	84	79
methionine	29	30	26
isoleucine	59	51	51
leucine	110	105	119
tyrosine	25	22	23
phenylalanine	42	41	45
trytophan	ND	ND	8
Total residues	1080	1076	1085

3 The Properties of Phytochrome

3.1 Photoconversion

The photoconversion of Pr → Pfr and of Pfr → Pr are both first order reactions (Fig. 3–1). This means that, at constant fluence rate (N), the rate of conversion of Pr to Pfr at a given time (t) is proportional to the amount of Pr remaining at that time.

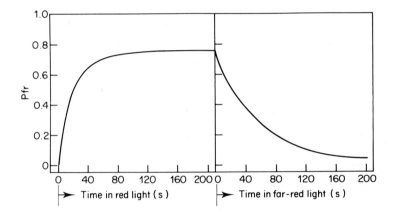

Fig. 3–1 Photoconversion of phytochrome showing first order kinetics. Light irradiance 3 W m^{-2} (13 μmol m^{-2}s^{-1} for red light and 12 μmol m^{-2}s^{-1} for far-red light).

$$\frac{dPr}{dt} = - \sigma.N.Pr$$

It follows that there is a linear relationship between the logarithm of Pr remaining and the fluence (Nt) given.

$$\ln \frac{Pr}{Pr_0} = - \sigma Nt$$

The gradient of the line is the photoconversion action constant (σ). This is the product of the extinction coefficient (ϵ) and the quantum yield (Φ see § 1.3). It can be calculated very simply from the time for half maximum photoconversion ($t_{1/2}$).

$$\sigma = 2.3\,\epsilon\,\Phi = \frac{\ln 2}{Nt_{1/2}}$$

The photoconversion constants, σ_1 for Pr → Pfr and σ_2 for Pfr → Pr, are, of course, wavelength dependent. Being a photochemical reaction the rate of conversion of phytochrome from one form to the other is relatively insensitive to temperature.

Although the Pr form of phytochrome absorbs very little in the far-red (F) region of the spectrum, the absorption spectra of Pr and Pfr overlap considerably in the red (R) region. This means that there is continuous interconversion of Pr and Pfr with a dynamic photostationary equilibrium. It is therefore impossible to obtain pure Pfr by irradiation of Pr, the absorption spectrum of R-irradiated phytochrome shown in Fig. 2–9 being that of a mixture of Pfr and Pr. The photostationary equilibria (Pfr/P=φ, where P is the total amount of phytochrome) can be calculated from photoconversion kinetics and absorption data. In this way R was shown to maintain 80% if

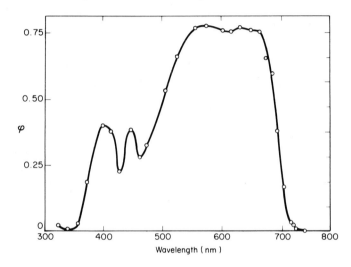

Fig. 3–2   Photostationary equilibrium (φ=Pfr/P) maintained by different wavelengths of light in mustard hypocotyls. (Redrawn from Hanke, J., Hartmann, K. M. and Mohr, H. (1969). *Planta*, **86**, 235.)

phytochrome in the Pfr form (φ=0.08) whereas F maintains less than 5% Pfr (φ<0.05). More recent calculations have indicated that the value for R-irradiated pure phytochrome in solutions is probably 0.75 (Fig. 3–2). Note that φ is independent of irradiance and is equal to $\sigma_1(\sigma_1+\sigma_2)$.

$$Pr \underset{N\sigma_2}{\overset{N\sigma_1}{\rightleftharpoons}} Pfr$$

The σ_1 and σ_2 values for 660 nm are respectively about 3000 and 1000 mol^{-1} m^2.

The amount of Pfr produced by a non-saturating dose of light can be calculated as follows.

$$Pfr = (1 - e^{-\sigma_r N t}) \varphi P$$

Although the photoconversion of one form of phytochrome to the other is a simple first order reaction it is not a single step process. The actual photoreaction, which presumably involves an isomeric change of the chromophore, is only the first step and is followed by a series of dark reactions before conversion is complete. The nature of these reactions and the intermediates between Pr and Pfr have been investigated by several techniques. Flash photolysis enables very rapid changes (less than a ms) in absorption to be measured. The data obtained using this technique show that after exposing Pr to a R flash, several intermediate stages are passed through before Pfr is formed. A similar situation was observed for the reverse reaction. Low temperature studies have also provided useful information about phytochrome intermediates. At the temperature of liquid nitrogen ($-196°C$) conversion of Pr to Pfr and vice-versa is not possible, although intermediates are formed. Raising the temperature results in intermediates further along the pathways to Pfr and Pr respectively being formed. A scheme based on studies of phytochrome using both these techniques *in vivo* and *in vitro* is shown in Fig. 3–3. Data from studies on freeze-dried (dehydrated) phytochrome are consistent with this scheme. In the dehydrated state Pr can be photoconverted to lumi-R but the presence of water is necessary for the subsequent reactions since they involve changes in protein conformation. Although at room temperature the dark reactions are completed within a few seconds of the photoreaction, intermediates can be present in significant proportions. This is the case under

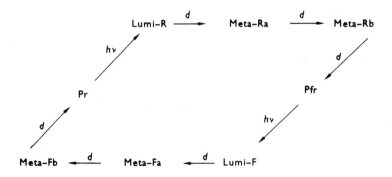

Fig. 3–3 Scheme proposed for the photoconversion of phytochrome. hv =photo-reaction; d =dark reaction. Approximate absorption peaks: lumi-R 698 nm; lumi-F, (? 650 or 720 nm); meta-Ra, 710 nm; meta-Fa, probably a complex, all red absorbing; meta-Rb and meta-Fb are relatively weakly absorbing. (Redrawn from Kendrick, R. E. and Spruit, C. J. P. (1973). *Plant Physiol.*, **52**, 327.)

mixed R/F light which excites both Pr and Pfr and so results in a continual cycling of the pigment. Under these conditions the dark reactions are important since they are the slowest point in the cycle. Therefore intermediates in the Pr → Pfr pathway accumulate, because these precede the slowest dark reaction (meta-Rb → Pfr). The intermediate meta-Rb is weakly absorbing compared to Pr or Pfr.

The nature of the chromophore isomerization is of great interest. The photoreaction at low temperature, e.g. Pr → lumi-R, is probably restricted to events within the chromophore and the dark reactions that occur at higher temperatures involve changes in both the chromophore and the protein. The protein changes are small relative to the overall molecular size of 120 000 daltons, but are no doubt of great significance at the 'active site' of the molecule.

Immunologically Pr and Pfr are identical, yet subtle differences have been found between Pr and Pfr. Small changes in ultra-violet light absorption for example, indicate a conformation change in the protein in the vicinity of the chromophore. This is confirmed by the availability of two or more lysine residues in Pr than in Pfr for reaction with glutaraldehyde. Recently Song and his co-workers, on the basis of differential reactivity of Pr and Pfr to several reagents have proposed that upon phototransformation of Pr to Pfr the chromophore folds out from a hydrophobic crevice to reveal a hydrophobic area on the protein (Fig. 3–4). Such a site could enable Pfr to react with other cell components, such as other proteins or membranes, and is of great interest when we consider the molecular mode of phytochrome action.

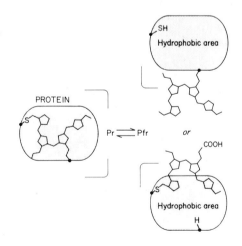

Fig. 3–4   Hahn and Song have proposed that upon phototransformation of Pr to Pfr the chromophore becomes exposed revealing a hydrophobic area (Redrawn from Hahn, T–R and Song P–S (1981). *Biochemistry*, **20**, 2062.)

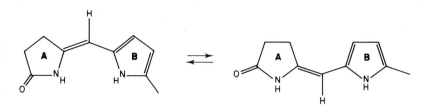

Fig. 3–5 A possible configuration change that is involved in phytochrome phototransformation.

The structure of the chromophore is now generally accepted to be that shown in Fig. 2–1, but the exact configuration and conformation is still a matter of speculation. The photo-isomerization of the chromophore in the interconversion of Pr and Pfr could possibly involve a configuration change about the double bond in the bridge linking rings A and B (Fig. 3–5). A comparison of the absorption spectra of Pr, Pfr, and intermediates with those predicted for theoretical tetrapyrrole structures has provided information about the chromophore during conversion. Both Pr and Pfr correspond to extended forms of the tetrapyrrole molecule, whereas the intermediate meta-Rb corresponds to a tightly folded form.

Phytochrome is photochromic, that is changes colour on exposure to light, and photoreversible. There is evidence of other photoreversible photochromic pigments in living organisms. In some fungi morphogenetic changes (e.g. conidiospore development in *Altenaria*) are induced by ultra-violet light and these effects can be reversed by blue light. This so-called *mycochrome* system may involve two different but closely associated pigments. Certain cyano-bacteria (blue-green algae) such as *Fremyella* show 'chromatic adaption' in their accessary photosynthetic pigments with green light increasing the formation of the green absorbing phycoerythrin and R increasing the formation of the R-absorbing phycocyanin. There are green-R reversible effects on growth and morphogenesis as well as on phycobilin formation. There is spectrophotometric evidence of the presence of a number of green-R reversible pigments in extracts. These are probably phycobiliproteins, chemically similar to phycoerythrin, phycocyanin and phytochrome, and have been referred to as *phycochromes* by Björn.

The visual pigment rhodopsin exhibits photoreversibility at low temperatures ($< -140°C$) with absorption maxima at 498 and 543 nm. Photo-conversion of rhodopsin (Fig. 3–6) involves a cis-trans isomerization in the chromophore which is followed by a series of dark reactions leading to a separation of chromophore (retinal) and protein (opsin). These end products reform rhodopsin by an enzymic reaction. The photoreversibility of rhodopsin can occur in the isolated chromophore whereas the phytochrome chromophore loses photoreversibility when detached from the protein.

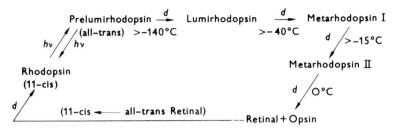

Fig. 3–6   The visual pigment rhodopsin undergoes a photoreversible reaction at low temperature.   At   higher   temperatures   the   photoproduct   of   rhodopsin (prelumirhodopsin) undergoes a series of dark reactions to form retinal plus opsin.

3.2   Dark reactions

A great deal of work has been carried out on the dark reactions of phytochrome both *in vivo* and *in vitro*. Figure 3–7 summarizes the reactions that have been observed *in vivo*. Phytochrome is found in seedlings grown in

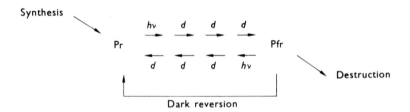

Fig. 3–7   Summary of the reaction of phytochrome *in vivo*.

the dark in the stable Pr form. The Pfr form is relatively unstable and *in vivo* following conversion from Pr by R it undergoes a process called *destruction* or decay. Destruction appears to be a real loss of phytochrome, since a similar decrease is observed by immunocytochemistry. The process requires oxygen and can be inhibited by metabolic inhibitors such as sodium azide. Under continuous R the quantity of phytochrome decreases by this process to a low level. On falling below a critical value more phytochrome is synthesised *de novo* in the Pr form and an equilibrium is reached between synthesis and destruction. Pfr can undergo another reaction, the thermal dark reversion to Pr. This reaction was first predicted on the basis of physiological experiments (see § 4.6). It takes place in all the dicotyledons so far investigated except for members of the Centrospermae. However, it is absent from most monocotyledons so far investigated. Figure 3–8 shows the changes in phytochrome levels which take place in the dark following conversion of Pr to Pfr by R. The situation in sunflower (*Helianthus annuus*) which exhibits dark reversion is compared with that in love-lies-bleeding (*Amaranthus caudatus*) where only

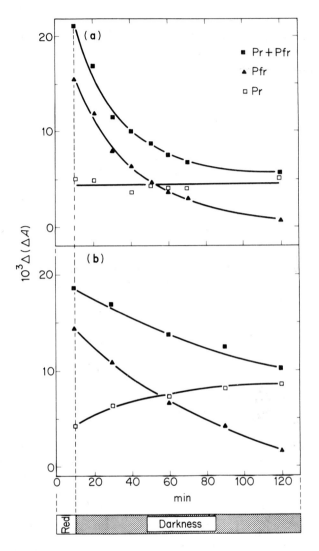

Fig. 3–8 The dark reactions of phytochrome after 10 min red light at 25°C (**a**) *Amaranthus* seedlings: demonstrates the process of destruction of Pfr and absence of dark reversion of Pfr to Pr. (Redrawn from Kendrick, R. E. and Frankland, B. (1969). *Planta*, **86**, 21.) (**b**) Sunflower hypocotyls: demonstrates that Pfr destruction and dark reversion of Pfr to Pr occur simultaneously. (By courtesy of Glynn, P. J. and Frankland, B.)

destruction takes place. Both destruction and dark reversion are temperature dependent.

The kinetics of Pfr destruction can be best studied in those species lacking dark reversion. In the dark, after a short exposure to R, Pfr destruction follows first order kinetics with the rate of destruction at any given time (t) being proportional to the amount of Pfr remaining at that time.

$$\frac{dPfr}{dt} = -kPfr$$

Integrating this becomes:

$$Pfr = Pfr_0 e^{-kt}$$

Written in the logarithmic form:

$$\ln \frac{Pfr}{Pfr_0} = -kt$$

Plotting the amount of Pfr on a logarithmic scale against time gives a straight line of gradient (k), the destruction rate constant of Pfr. At 25°C, k is 0.037 min^{-1} in *Amaranthus* seedlings corresponding to a half-life ($t_{1/2}$) of about 20 min.

$$t_{1/2} = \frac{\ln 2}{k}$$

Rates of destruction are rather slower in other species. For instance, in sunflower there is a half-life of about 50 min at 25°C. Where dark reversion and destruction occur together analysis of the kinetics is more difficult. In most cases the results are not explained by assuming two simple first order reactions competing for Pfr.

The time course curves of phytochrome destruction under continuous irradiation are also exponential in form and in all cases there is a linear relationship between the logarithm of phytochrome concentration and time. The rate of disappearance of phytochrome at any time is proportional to the concentration of the unstable Pfr form at that time. Since the re-establishment of the photochemical equilibrium between Pr and Pfr is very rapid compared to destruction of Pfr, then under continuous irradiation the rate of decay of total phytochrome (P) will be given by the equation:

$$dP = -\frac{k\varphi P}{dt}$$

where k is the rate constant for destruction of Pfr and ϕ is the proportion of the phytochrome in the Pfr form (Pfr/P). The equation can be written in the logarithmic form thus:

$$\ln \frac{P}{P_0} = k\varphi t$$

When $\ln P/P_0$ is plotted against time the gradient of the line is $k\varphi$, the rate constant for destruction of total phytochrome. Plotting this against φ gives a straight line with gradient equal to k. Conversely φ can be calculated by determining the $k\varphi$ value graphically and dividing by k. Kinetics of this kind can be used in estimating Pfr/P ratios under various light treatments. This is especially useful with continuous F where the amount of Pfr is very low and accurate measurement is not possible by direct spectrophotometry.

Pfr destruction in monocotyledonous seedlings, such as those of oats (*Avena sativa*), follows zero order kinetics, i.e. there is a linear relationship between Pfr remaining and time. The rate of destruction is not dependent on the amount of Pfr present and is almost as rapid under continuous F as under continuous R. Even in dicotyledonous seedlings there is evidence for destruction being more complex. For instance, at low phytochrome levels destruction appears to occur at a much slower rate. Also, deviation from simple kinetics has been observed at high fluence rates. Pr destruction has also been observed, but this is restricted to Pr that has been cycled through the Pfr form.

Dark reversion of Pfr to Pr has been observed in extracts of most species. Interestingly those species lacking the process *in vivo* such as the monocotyledons readily demonstrate the process *in vitro*. Low pH and a low oxidation-reduction potential enhance the process. It has been suggested that the presence of this reaction *in vivo* is correlated with the immediate environment of the phytochrome molecules. This is not the only change in properties that occurs upon extraction. The peak absorbance of Pfr shifts about 10 nm to a shorter wavelength. This change *in vitro* is probably associated with proteolytic degradation of the native phytochrome molecule (see § 2.6). It is possible that the different *in vivo* properties are due to a close association between phytochrome and other molecules such as membrane components.

Phytochrome *in vitro* can easily be denatured by other compounds such as urea. Under these conditions Pfr forms a compound of much lower absorbance while still retaining photoreversibility. Denaturation can therefore be measured using the ratio of the absorbance change at the peak of Pfr (730 nm) to that at the peak of Pr (660 nm) following photoconversion. $\Delta A730/\Delta A660$ is equal to one for native phytochrome but less than one for denatured phytochrome.

Another reaction observed *in vitro* is the phenomenon of R enhanced 'pelletability' of phytochrome. If a crude homogenate of a dark grown tissue is placed in a centrifuge tube and spun at low speed, most of the phytochrome remains in the supernatant at a pH above 7.0. However, if the tissue is pre-irradiated with R before homogenization, a larger proportion of phytochrome is observed in the pellet. In some systems Mg^{2+} is necessary for the R enhancement of 'pelletability'. This process has been studied like any other phytochrome response. It is only reversible if F immediately follows a short flash of R. This process is one of the most rapid phytochrome responses observed to date. Since the pellet contains a myriad of components, including organelles and membranes, it is impossible to be absolutely sure to what phytochrome is associating. Nevertheless, the process appears to be a function of Pfr and could well have some significance to the understanding of the localization of phytochrome in the cell and its physiological function. Although the association of Pfr with the pellet has not been fully characterized it could reflect interaction of the hydrophobic site on Pfr (Fig. 3–4) with a protein or membrane constituent. Since phytochrome (Pr) is readily solubilized it appears that in darkness phytochrome is a soluble protein or a peripheral membrane protein, a conclusion supported by immunocytochemistry (Fig. 2–9). Pfr on the other hand appears to be more tenaciously bound to membranes and organelles. An interesting observation revealed by immunocytochemistry is the marked change in distribution of phytochrome upon irradiation of dark-grown tissue with R. This involves a loss of the homogeneous distribution typical of dark grown material to yet unidentified discrete areas of the cell (Fig. 2–9). This phenomenon has been called 'sequestering' and has only been observed in a few species and it is not known if it is a general phenomenon. Whatever its significance this reaction is a very rapid phytochrome response occurring within a few seconds at physiological temperatures.

3.3 Biosynthesis

The concentration of phytochrome in dry seeds is very low and usually not detectable. On addition of water the level of detectable phytochrome increases rapidly. This increases appears to be the result of the hydration of phytochrome molecules that are already present but do not show photo-reversibility in the dehydrated state (Fig. 3–9). After a period the amount of phytochrome then increases again. This second increase has been shown by density labelling techniques to result from the *de novo* synthesis of phytochrome in the Pr form. This increase corresponds to the time of germination of the seeds and continues during seedling development until a plateau is reached. There is some evidence to support the idea that this does not represent a cessation of synthesis but rather a balance between Pr synthesis and Pr degradation. If total phytochrome is reduced by Pfr destruction, which must be a more rapid process than Pr degradation, a subsequent rise in phytochrome level can be observed in the dark. Under continuous irradiation a balance is eventually reached between destruction and synthesis (Fig. 3–10).

3.4 Phytochrome in light grown plants

Norflurazon treatment of light-grown plants (see § 2.3) has enabled phytochrome to be measured by spectrophotometry, despite the low levels

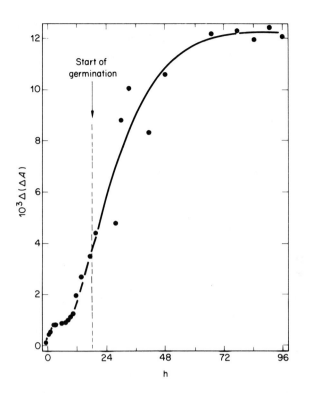

Fig. 3–9 Time course of phytochrome appearance in *Amaranthus* seed from the time of sowing in darkness at 25°C. (Redrawn from Kendrick, R. E., Spruit, C. J. P. and Frankland, B. (1969). *Planta*, **88**, 293.)

present. In some cases reduced rates of synthesis and destruction have been observed, compared to etiolated seedlings. Spectrophotometric investigations of white flower petals and the white regions of variegated leaves have also revealed low levels of phytochrome. One tissue from light-grown plants which is fairly high in phytochrome is cauliflower (*Brassica oleracea*) curd. In this case the phytochrome appears to be really photostable since on irradiation with R there is no Pfr destruction but only dark reversion to Pr.

Extraction from light grown plants has been successful although rarely attempted. One estimate of phytochrome content on the basis of extraction from light grown plants is 200–300 ng g^{-1} fresh weight compared to 5 μg g^{-1} fresh weight in etiolated seedlings. In plants grown under day/night cycles the radioimmunoassay (see § 2.4) has been used to demonstrate that the level of phytochrome falls during the day and rises during the night, confirming that the destruction and synthesis reactions occur in green, light-grown plants.

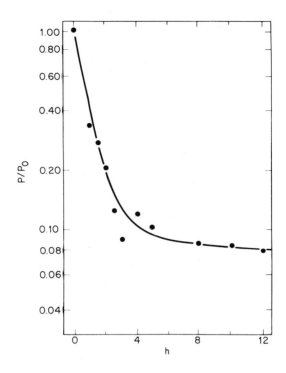

Fig. 3–10 Changes in total phytochrome in *Amaranthus* seedlings under continuous irradiation with red light at 25°C. Phytochrome as a proportion of that present initially (P/P_0) plotted on a logarithmic scale against time. Demonstrates that a balance is eventually reached between destruction and synthesis. (Redrawn Kendrick, R. E. Spruit, C. J. P. and Frankland, B. (1969). *Planta*, **88**, 293.)

3.5 Phylogenetic aspects

Physiological responses suggest that phytochrome is present throughout the plant kingdom, from green algae up to the higher land plants. R–F reversible photoresponses have been demonstrated in fungi and in red algae and there is some evidence of R–F reversible absorbance changes although the presence of phytochrome has not been proved conclusively. In photosynthetic organisms the possible involvement of chlorophyll must always be considered as R–F antagonism could arise through differential excitation of photosystems I and II. Positive identification of phytochrome by spectrophotometry or isolation has only been observed in a few lower plants. One striking difference appears to have been found between higher and some lower plants. The absorption peaks of Pr and Pfr are shifted to shorter wavelengths in the green alga *Maesotaenium* and the bryophyte *Sphaerocarpus* (Table 2). *In vivo* measurements of phytochrome in several gymnosperms (e.g. pine) similarly show absorption shifts to shorter wavelengths.

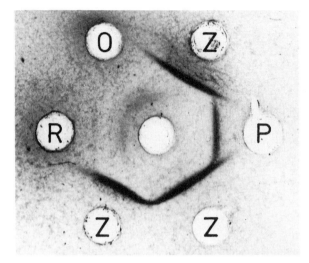

Fig. 3–11 Comparison of oat (0), rye (R), pea (P) and zucchini squash (Z) by the Ouchterlony double diffusion agar plate technique against antizucchini squash phytochrome (centre well). After diffusion, protein immunoprecipitates stained with Coomassie blue before photography. The zucchini squash antibody shows only partial recognition of pea phytochrome and very poor recognition of oat and rye phytochromes. (From Cordonnier, M–M, and Pratt, L. H. (1980). In *Photoreceptors and Plant Development*, p. 69. Ed. J. De Greef, University Press, Antwerp.)

As mentioned in section 3.2 a relationship between *in vivo* dark reversion and taxonomy has been found in the species investigated. Dark reversion is absent in most monocotyledons and one order of dicotyledons, the Centrospermae. The latter group also shows other unique biochemical features.

Despite their spectral similarity, phytochrome in monocotyledons and dicotyledons differ immunologically. The antibody to the dicotyledon zucchini squash (*Cucurbita pepo*) phytochrome shows only partial recognition of dicotyledon phytochrome from pea (*Pisum sativum*) and a very poor recognition for phytochrome from the monocotyledons oat (*Avena sativa*) and rye (*Secale cereale*) (Fig. 3–11). Clearly there has been evolution of the phytochrome protein. Presumably the region of the protein in the vicinity of the chromophore has been highly conserved, since this is the functional part of the molecule involved in its mechanism of action. Only when more complete data are available will a clear evolutionary record of phytochrome emerge. Obviously phytochrome evolved at an early stage and its present ubiquitous distribution points to its success as a control system.

Table 2   Absorption characteristics of phytochrome *in vivo* and *in vitro*.

	Group	Genus	Absorbance maxima (nm) Pr	Pfr
In vivo	Angiosperms	*Avena*	665	735
		Pisum	665	732
	Gymnosperms	*Pinus*	656	714
	Pteridophytes	*Anemia*	662	737
In vitro	Angiosperms	*Avena*	660	725
		Pisum	665	725
	Bryophytes	*Sphaerocarpus*	655	720
		Mnium	658	724
	Algae	*Maesotaenium*	649	710

4 Phytochrome Controlled Responses

4.1 Photoresponses

Phytochrome is the receptor pigment involved in many developmental responses of plants to light. It acts as a simple light detector and as a sensor of light quality, and probably light quantity, as well as being involved, less directly, in measurement of light duration. The regulatory effects of light on growth and development are seen most dramatically at two stages in the life cycle of the plant. Firstly, at the stage of seed germination and seedling development, and secondly at the stage of transition from the vegetative to the flowering phase (see § 1.1).

All seedlings show developmental responses to light. These are associated with the transition from a seedling, dependent on food reserves and adapted for easy passage upwards through the soil, to a young plant with photosynthetic leaves. The morphological changes involved in this transition differ from species to species. For instance, in many dicotyledonous seedlings, such as sunflower (*Helianthus annuus*) or mustard (*Sinapis alba*), shoot extension in the dark is chiefly associated with the hypocotyl (Fig. 4–1). The upper part of the hypocotyl is in the form of a hook, the shoot apex and cotyledons pointing downwards and so being protected from damage as the seedling grows up through the soil. The effect of light is to inhibit hypocotyl elongation, to cause unfolding of the hypocotyl hook and to induce expansion of the cotyledons. Apart from the obvious synthesis of chlorophyll a variety of structural and physiological changes take place within the cotyledon as part of the transition from a storage organ to a photosynthetic leaf. In contrast to this type of seedling development some species, such as pea (*Pisum sativum*), show very little longitudinal extension of the hypocotyl, the cotyledons remaining below ground level (Fig. 4–1). Extension growth is the result of elongation of the first internodes. In seedlings grown in the dark there is again a terminal hook region protecting the shoot apex and very little leaf expansion. Light inhibits extension of the first internode, promotes extension of later internodes, causes hook unfolding and promotes expansion of the young leaves.

In graminaceous seedlings, such as oats (*Avena sativa*), there is no terminal hook but the young leaves are sheathed and protected by a modified leaf, the coleoptile (Fig. 4–1). The cotyledon remains within the seed and serves to absorb food materials from the endosperm. During the early stages of development of an oat seedling light inhibits extension of the first internode but promotes extension of the coleoptile. Although leaves are formed and grow in the dark they are tightly rolled. Light induces leaf unrolling as well as chlorophyll formation and differentiation of etioplasts to chloroplasts. Not all

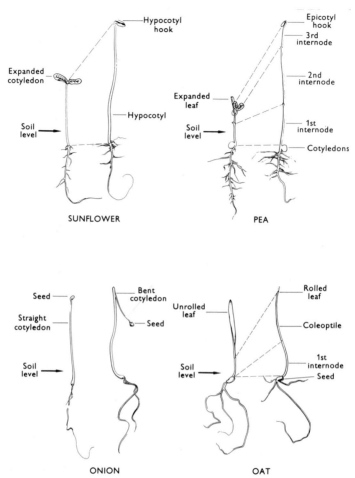

Fig. 4–1 Photomorphogenesis in seedlings. *Left:* Light-grown. *Right:* Dark-grown.

monocotyledons show this type of seedling development. In onion (*Allium cepa*), for instance, there is a narrow, elongated cotyledon, the tip of which is embeded in the endosperm of the seed (Fig. 4–1). Elongation of this cotyledon carries the seed above ground level. The cotyledon is bent at an acute angle and like the dicotyledonous hypocotyl shows a straightening response to light.

Not only does light have marked effects on seedling development but seed germination may also be affected by light. In many species germination is stimulated by light whereas in other species germination is inhibited by light. These effects of light may be seen both as changes in the proportion of seeds germinating and as changes in the time taken for seeds to germinate. The effect of light is frequently temperature dependent. For instance, lettuce (*Lactuca sativa*) seeds may germinate readily in both light and dark at 15°C, will germinate in neither light nor dark at 35°C but at 25°C show a low germination response in the dark with a marked positive response to light. In the light-inhibited seeds of love-lies-bleeding (*Amaranthus caudatus*) the temperature response is reversed with germination being favoured by high rather than low temperatures. A light requirement for germination is particularly characteristic of weed species such as charlock (*Sinapis arvensis*), white goosefoot (*Chenopodium album*), dock (*Rumex obtusifolius*) and plantain (*Plantago major*). Such seeds tend not to germinate whilst buried in the soil but do so when exposed at the surface by cultivation.

The length of the day is one of the most important environmental variables determining the time of year when a particular species comes into flower (see § 1.1). Long day plants (LDP) such as henbane (*Hyoscyamus niger*) flower when the days are longer than some critical length; SDP such as cocklebur (*Xanthium strumarium*) flower when the days are shorter than some critical length. Plants may show a 'quantitative' response to the length of the day. For instance, a LDP such as lettuce or rye-grass (*Lolium*) flowers most rapidly under long days but will eventually come into flower even under short days. In the case of cocklebur a single short day will induce flowering in plants which have been returned to non-inductive long days. This phenomenon of photoperiodism is found in relation to other aspects of plant development. For instance, the formation of dormant buds in many temperate-zone trees such as sycamore maple (*Acer pseudoplatanus*) is induced by short days. Although a period of high light is necessary for most photoperiodic responses there is evidence that the most important factor is the length of the dark period. If the long dark period of a short day is interrupted by light a long day response will be produced (Fig. 1–2). Such light-break treatments are made use of commercially in maintaining glasshouse-grown *Chrysanthemum* plants (Fig. 4–2), a SDP, in the vegetative stage during autumn and winter. Plants can be brought into flower by terminating the light-break treatment. During the summer *Chrysanthemum* plants remain vegetative but can be brought into flower by covering them with black polythene in the morning and evening and so artificially shortening the day. It is now known that the length of the uninterupted dark period is not the only controlling factor in photoperiodism. There is increasing evidence that the duration, irradiance and quality of light during the light period can have effects on the flowering response. Also it has been shown in some species that during an artificially long dark period there is a rhythmic change in the response to a light break (see § 4.10). Interruptions of the dark period after 24 and 48 h tend to promote flowering in SDP whereas interruptions after 36 and 60 h tend to inhibit flowering.

4.2   The classical red/far-red reversible reaction

Phytochrome is assumed to be the receptor pigment where induction of a response by a short irradiation with red (R) light can be reversed by a

Fig. 4–2 Photoperiodic control of flowering in *Chrysanthemum* cv Polaris. Plants grown under long days (left) or short days (right). Scale divisions 10 cm. (By courtesy of Cockshull, K. E., copyright Glasshouse Crops Research Institute, Littlehampton, Sussex.)

subsequent irradiation with far-red (F) light. This is the classical R–F reversible situation although phytochrome may be involved in other kinds of photo-responses. Action spectra show a peak for induction at 660 nm and a peak for reversion of this at 730 nm. These action peaks correspond to the peaks of absorption of Pr and Pfr respectively (see § 1.2). R–F reversible responses have been observed in many aspects of seedling photomorphogenesis, including growth, structural and biosynthetic changes. R–F reversibility is a feature of light stimulated seed germination in several species and of the light break in photoperiodic effects on flowering (see § 1.1). R–F reversible responses have also been found in lower plants such as ferns (e.g. spore germination in *Osmunda*), mosses (e.g. phototropism in protonemata of *Physcomitrella*), liverworts (e.g. thallus growth in *Marchantia*) and green algae (e.g. chloroplast orientation in *Mougeotia*). R–F reversible responses have also been found in red algae (e.g. photoperiodic induction of sporangia formation in the filamentous phase of *Porphyra*) and fungi (e.g. carotenoid formation in

Verticillium) although the involvement of phytochrome has not been proved conclusively.

4.3   Rate of response and relationship between response and quantity of light

A short period of R induces a response which takes place in the dark sometime after the exposure to light. In the case of R induced growth of apical buds in pea seedlings there is a lag period of about 4 h before there is a measurable difference between irradiated seedlings and those maintained continuously in the dark. In the case of light induced germination of lettuce seeds the response time at 25°C is about 12 h. Some responses, however, are very rapid, an example being the nyctinastic closing movement of the leaflets of the sensitive plant (*Mimosa pudica*). Leaves transferred from light to dark show a closing response after 5 min and complete closing within 30 min. The response is prevented by a short exposure to F before the leaves are transferred to the dark.

Responses can be induced by very small amounts of light. Figure 4–3 shows the fluence-response relationship for R light inhibition of first internode extension in oat (*Avena sativa*) seedlings. The response is proportional to the logarithm of incident light energy and is saturated at 100 J m^{-2}. This quantity of light would be contained in about 2 s of normal sunlight! In fact the oat first internode will show a small but significant response to 0.1 J m^{-2}. This amount of light is sufficient to saturate very sensitive systems such as the hook opening response in bean seedlings!

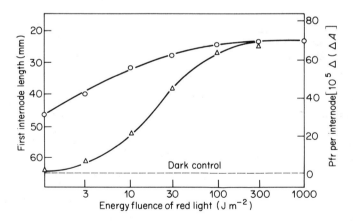

Fig. 4–3 Fluence-response relationship for red light inhibition of first internode extension (O) and Pfr formation (Δ) in oat seedlings. (Redrawn from Loercher, L. (1966). *Plant Physiol.*, **41**, 932.)

4.4   Quantitative relationship between response and Pfr

R may have promoting or inhibiting effects. For instance, in pea (*Pisum sativum*) seedlings R inhibits the extension of the first internode but promotes leaf expansion. It is possible to think of all R effects as positive. Light inhibits cell extension by promoting cell maturation.

The primary effect of R is to convert Pr to Pfr. Is the inhibition of internode extension due to the presence of Pfr or to the absence of Pr? In other words, is Pfr the physiologically active form of phytochrome? The data in Fig. 4–3 can be re-plotted to show that there is a simple linear relationship between the response and the logarithm of the amount of Pfr (Fig. 4–4). A change in the Pfr/P ratio from say, 0.01 to 0.05 produces a large response. The concurrent change in Pr/P ratio is from 0.99 to 0.95. If Pr were the active form it is difficult to see why a small relative change in Pr should produce such a large response. On the basis of circumstantial evidence of this kind Pfr is taken to be the physiologically active form of phytochrome.

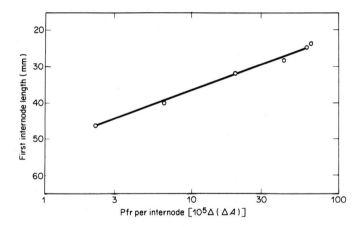

Fig. 4–4   Red light inhibition of first internode extension in oat seedlings as a function of Pfr. Data as for Fig. 4–3. Pfr plotted on a logarithmic scale. (Redrawn from Loercher, L. (1966). *Plant Physiol.*, **41**, 932.)

Figure 4–4 shows a simple relationship between response and Pfr in oat (*Avena sativa*) seedlings. Figure 4–5 gives data for light inhibition of extension of pea stem sections. Stem sections were exposed for 15 min to various mixtures of R and F establishing various photostationary states. Here again the response is related to Pfr/P ratio although values of 0.5 and above are saturating. These are *graded* responses to Pfr in contrast to an ungraded or *threshold* response as shown by Mohr and co-workers in the light inhibition of lipoxygenase formation in mustard cotyledons. Light giving a Pfr/P ratio greater than 0.01 completely inhibits lipoxygenase formation whereas light giving a Pfr/P ratio less than 0.01 has no effect on the level of enzyme activity. In this system it can be shown that the response is related to the absolute amount or concentration of Pfr and not to the proportion of phytochrome in the Pfr form. However, there are other responses which are not quantitatively related to the absolute amount of Pfr and it has been argued that the ratio between Pfr and Pr molecules is important in determining such responses.

If the experiment with pea stem sections, described above, is repeated with sections from seedlings that were irradiated 9 h previously with R the data shown in Fig. 4–6 are obtained. F which establishes about 5% of phytochrome in the Pfr form, now promotes elongation, presumably by reversing Pfr to Pr. There is no effect of light producing 30% Pfr suggesting that the tissue already contains 30% Pfr. However, spectrophotometric measurements show that this is not so. Pfr is unstable and in the dark either undergoes destruction or dark reversion to Pr (see § 3.2). This situation, where spectrophotometry fails to confirm the presence of Pfr which has been deduced from physiological responses to light, has been described by Hillman as a 'phytochrome paradox'. One explanation is that there is a small 'pool' of physiologically active phytochrome, distinct from the 'bulk' phytochrome, which is relatively stable and persists in the dark for a relatively long period. On the other hand it has been proposed by Kendrick and Spruit that all phytochrome is active and controls specific responses by virtue of its localization in particular molecular environments within the cell, where its properties may be significantly different.

4.5   Transmissible phytochrome effects

Plant hormones, such as auxins and gibberellins, are involved in the internal regulation of plant growth and it seems probable that some phytochrome controlled responses involve changes in the level of such hormones. A R–F reversible response may take place in one part of the plant following irradiation of another part. For instance, in bean seedlings irradiation of the hypocotyl hook region with R can induce expansion of the young leaves. Clearly there is transmission of a stimulus. Some transmissible phytochrome effects may be mediated by hormones but in this particular example the rate of transmission is too rapid for this to be a likely explanation.

Leaf unrolling in cereals can be induced by R and can also be brought about by gibberellin treatment in the dark. It has been demonstrated that in etioplasts isolated from dark-grown cereal leaves there is a rapid increase in extractable gibberellin following exposure to R. This appears to involve existing gibberellin as well as conversion of a basic 'bound' gibberellin into an acid 'free' gibberellin. Although gibberellin treatment will induce germination in light-requiring seeds there is no direct evidence for phytochrome controlled changes in endogenous gibberellins. However, in some seeds R irradiation causes rapid cytokinin changes, butanol soluble cytokinins increasing with water soluble cytokinin ribotides and ribosides decreasing. In the flowering response there is transmission of a stimulus over a long distance from the leaves where day-length is perceived to the growing apex where floral primordia are formed. It

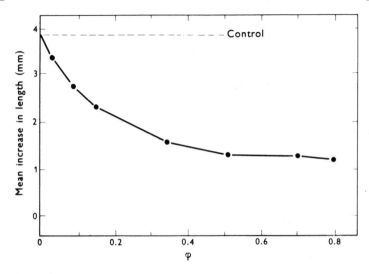

Fig. 4–5 Elongation of 5 mm stem sections from dark-grown pea seedlings following irradiation for 15 min with various mixtures of red and far-red light establishing different Pfr/P ratios (φ). (Redrawn from Hillman, W. S. (1965). *Physiol. Plant.* **18**, 346.)

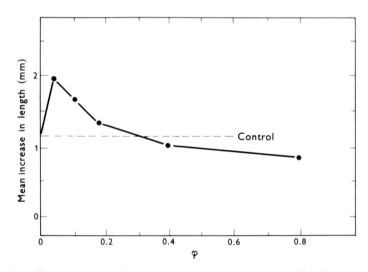

Fig. 4–6 Experiment as in Fig. 4–5, but stem sections from pea seedlings irradiated 9 h previously with red light. (Redrawn from Hillman, W. S. (1965). *Physiol. Plant*, **18**, 346.)

has been proposed that the flowering stimulus is a hormone, florigen, although it has not yet been isolated and identified.

4.6   Escape from reversibility: time course of Pfr action

If there is a sufficiently long dark period between irradiation with R and subsequent F there is loss of reversibility. Figure 4–7 presents data for R inhibition of coleoptile growth in intact rice (*Oryza sativa*) seedlings and shows the progressive loss of reversibility by F as the length of the intervening dark period is increased. There is 50% loss of reversibility after 8 h. Such 'escape curves' are of great interest in that they indicate the time course of Pfr action. During the dark period Pfr is active and although it can be reversed to Pr by F its action cannot be so reversed. The rate of escape from F reversibility is usually temperature dependent. For instance, in lettuce seed germination the time for 50% loss of reversibility is 9 h at 20°C and 5 h at 25°C. In the case of inhibition of flowering in the SDP cocklebur by a R interruption of the dark period, escape from F reversibility is completed within 30 min. This indicates rapid *potentiation* or *induction* of the response although the response itself is not rapid. It is three days before a change from a vegetative to a flowering apex is visible in plants exposed to a long night which was not interrupted by light.

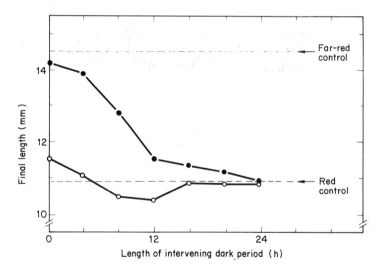

Fig. 4–7   Effect of intervening dark period between red and far-red light on escape of red light induction of inhibition of rice coleoptile elongation from far-red reversal at 27°C.   ●———●   Dark grown intact coleoptiles exposed to red light for 3 min and returned to darkness for various periods before exposure to far-red light for 3 min. ○———○   As above, but a second red irradiation given immediately after the far-red light. Final coleoptile length measured 2 days after first red irradiation. (Redrawn from Pjon, C. J. and Furuya, M. (1967). *Plant and Cell Physiol.*, **8**, 709.)

In photoperiodic control of flowering, R given at the end of the light period has no effect whereas R given in the middle of the dark period inhibits flowering in SDP and promotes flowering in LDP. R can only act by converting

Pr to Pfr and therefore phytochrome in the Pr form must have appeared during the dark period. This is taken as physiological evidence for the non-photochemical reversion of Pfr to Pr (see § 3.2).

In seedling growth responses it is often found that F does not completely reverse the effect of R. In such cases F alone usually produces the same response as R followed by F. The small but significant response is due to the small proportion (about 5%) of Pfr established by F. Almost full reversal of R induction can be obtained by using F of 750 or 760 nm. Incomplete reversal can also be due to rapid potentiation with some Pfr action taking place during the R irradiation period. In this case R followed by F will produce a larger response than F alone.

4.7   Requirement for repeated irradiation with red light

Prolonged irradiation with R may be necessary for certain responses. For example, many seeds require prolonged or intermittent irradiation for induction of germination. In the case of light inhibition of cucumber (*Cucumis sativus*) hypocotyl elongation the response can be induced by repeated short exposures to R over a period of time. The R irradiations are F reversible. There is clearly a need for Pfr action over a long period of time, possibly due to the supply of some 'reaction partner' limiting the response. Alternatively there may be a need for the accumulation of some product of Pfr action. Responses of this kind indicate that, following each R irradiation, there must be a fall in Pfr level (e.g. by dark reversion to Pr, or by Pfr destruction followed by Pr synthesis).

4.8   Far-red inhibition of seed germination

Some seeds, for instance those of certain varieties of tomato (*Solanum esculentum*), germinate in the dark but can be inhibited by a short exposure to F. This effect of F can be reversed by R. This suggests that phytochrome must be present as Pfr in such seeds in the dark. Since seeds normally develop in daylight it is surprising that so many contain only a low proportion of their phytochrome as Pfr. One possible explanation is that seeds may mature and dehydrate while still covered by green, chlorophyll containing fruit tissue which transmit F light more than R (see § 4.13).

Irradiation of dry seeds with R or white light will not normally induce germination chiefly because phytochrome in the dehydrated state cannot be transformed from Pr to Pfr. Phytochrome becomes fully photoreversible following imbition of water. However, dry seeds can be affected by F irradiation through removal of Pfr by conversion to meta-Fa (see § 3.1 and Fig. 3–3). This intermediate absorbs R and can be converted back to Pfr. This F–R reversibility in dry seeds is seen most clearly in seeds with an artificially high level of Pfr. Such seeds can be produced by allowing them to imbibe water in the dark, irradiating with R and then redrying.

Some seeds, such as those of *Amaranthus caudatus* and some varieties of lettuce, which germinate in the dark, require prolonged F irradiation to inhibit germination. Dormancy can be induced by 48h F irradiation but this can be broken by a single short R irradiation. This seems to indicate that Pfr is appearing in the seed in the dark over a long period of time. A possible explanation is that the seed phytochrome is not fully hydrated and on transfer of seeds from F to dark Pfr is formed from intermediates. However, many seeds may be prevented from germinating by prolonged exposure to high irradiance white light with a high φ value. This suggests that the inhibitory effects of prolonged F may arise for reasons other than the maintenance of a low Pfr level (see § 4.11).

In seed germination prolonged F irradiation acts in the opposite way to short R irradiation. In contrast, in seedling photomorphogenesis prolonged F irradiation acts in the same way as short R despite the fact that short F reverses the effect of short R (see § 4.11).

4.9 Phytochrome action in light-grown plants

It has already been mentioned that R–F reversibility can be demonstrated in relation to light interruption of the dark period in experiments on the photoperiodic control of flowering. This clearly shows that phytochrome is involved as a light detector in normal light-grown, green plants as well as in dark-grown seedlings and seeds sown in the dark.

Phytochrome can also be shown to be involved in the regulation of growth in light-grown plants. For instance, the elongation of stem internodes in bean plants grown under 8 h days can be increased four times by irradiating the plants with 5 min F at the end of the light period. The type of growth obtained depends on whether or not Pfr is present during the dark period.

There is also strong evidence that the proportion of phytochrome in the Pfr form during the main light period is important in regulating growth and morphogenesis. For instance, plants grown under light sources supplemented with F light often show striking stem elongation responses (see Fig. 4–8).

4.10 Phytochrome and biological time measurement

Photoperiodic responses must involve time measurement, particularly measurement of the length of the dark period. At first it was suggested that the dark reversion of Pfr to Pr must provide the basis of an 'hour glass' type of clock. However, the process is not temperature independent and for this and other reasons the idea was rejected. The existence of a number of rhythmic phenomena suggests that there is an oscillating type of 'biological clock'. Rhythms have been observed in the 'sleep movements' of leaves and in biochemical parameters such as carbon dioxide output, activities of various enzymes and levels of adenosine triphosphate (ATP). Such rhythms are described as *endogenous*, since they continue after transfer from normal light/dark cycles to constant environmental conditions, and *circadian*, since they

| R/F ratio | 2.28 | 0.61 | 0.32 | 0.18 |
| φ | 0.68 | 0.48 | 0.28 | 0.24 |

Fig. 4–8 Plants of *Chenopodium album* grown under artificial light source with the same amount of photosynthetically active radiation but supplemented with various amounts of far-red light. Light quality indicated by red/far-red (R/F) photon ratio and estimated Pfr/P (φ) ratio. (By courtesy of Smith, H. and Morgan, D. C. Leicester University.)

have a periodicity of approximately 24 h. Phytochrome has been implicated in the initiation and the phase-setting of such rhythms. In photoperiodism phytochrome may be involved in starting an oscillating system which measures the dark period. However, the clock may be independent of phytochrome but control changes in sensitivity to Pfr during the dark period (see § 4.1).

In both SDP and LDP Pfr has both inhibitory and promotory effects on flowering dependent upon the phase in the diurnal cycle when it is present. In the SDP Japanese morning glory (*Pharbitis nil*) flowering is inhibited by exposure to F at the beginning of a long inductive dark period whereas flowering is inhibited by R given 8 h after the end of the main light period (Fig. 4–9). This suggests that there is a dual role for phytochrome with reactions that depend on the presence of Pfr being followed by reactions which are inhibited by Pfr. LDP have a similar dual requirement except that their inductive reactions are out of phase with those of SDP. In LDP both the Pfr promoted and the Pfr inhibited reactions can be satisfied by continuous light containing both R and F and maintaining an intermediate level of Pfr.

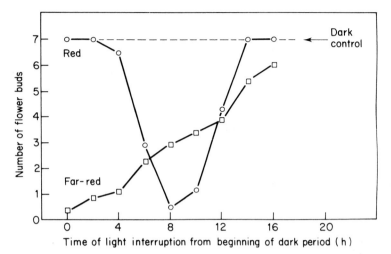

Fig. 4–9 Flowering response of *Pharbitis nil* to a single interruption with 5 min red or 5 min far-red ight given at different times during a 48 h dark period. Plants can be induced to flower by a single long dark period preceded and followed by continuous light. (Redrawn from Takimoto, A. and Hamner, K. C. (1965). *Plant Physiol.*, **40**, 859.)

4.11   The high irradiance reaction

Plants are not normally exposed to short periods of R and F light. Normally they are exposed to prolonged, high irradiance white light from the sun. Although a short exposure to R may induce marked changes in seedling development it does not transform a seedling into a normal looking green plant. Prolonged irradiation is necessary for this.

Figure 4–10 shows that for prolonged or continuous irradiation there are peaks of action in the blue and F regions of the spectrum. Prolonged F irradiation, unlike short F irradiation, acts in the same way as short R and is, in fact, more effective than prolonged R irradiation. Mohr has described this as the high energy reaction or *high irradiance reaction*. Originally it was suggested that there was a receptor pigment with absorption peaks in the blue and F regions of the spectrum but there are other explanations.

Hartmann investigated the high irradiance reaction using dual-wavelength experiments. The systems used were the photoinhibition of lettuce hypocotyl extension and the photoinhibition of lettuce germination. Both responses require prolonged irradiation and there is increasing response with increasing irradiance. In both cases there is a sharp peak of action at about 720 nm. It was found that the action of 720 nm light could be nullified if mixed with otherwise inactive light, either from the red or from the infra-red side of 720 nm. There was also an enhancement effect where action could be produced by an appropriate mixture of two otherwise inactive wavelengths (Fig. 4–11). Effects of this kind are difficult to interpret in terms of a pigment with a peak of

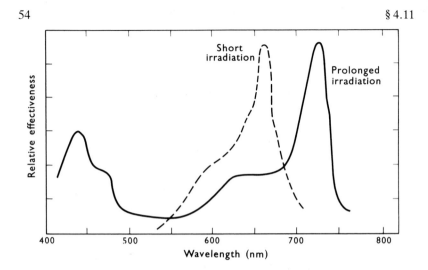

Fig. 4–10 Action spectra for effects of prolonged and short irradiations on seedling development. The two curves are plotted on different scales (short red is, of course, less effective than prolonged red irradiation). (Redrawn from Mohr, H. (1965). *Planta*, **53**, 219.)

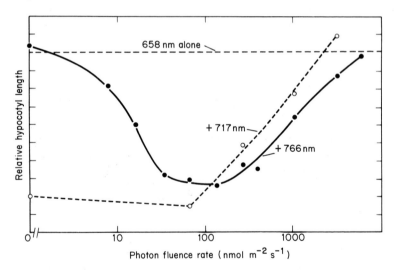

Fig. 4–11 Inhibition of hypocotyl elongation in lettuce seedlings under continuous simultaneous irradiation with different photon fluence rates at 658 nm and a constant high flux background of either 717 nm or 766 nm. (Redrawn from Hartmann, K. M. (1966). *Photochem. Photobiol.*, **5**, 349.)

absorption at 720 nm. They can be interpreted in terms of phytochrome if it is assumed that there is an optimal Pfr/P ratio for action. Maximum effect is obtained with a light mixture giving a φ value of about 0.1. One suggestion is that this arises because of the Pfr destruction process, the most effective light source being that which leads to the maximum amount of Pfr integrated over time. However, it can be demonstrated that an equilibrium is eventually established between the rate of Pr synthesis and the rate of Pfr destruction so that the absolute amount of Pfr (although not the Pfr/P ratio) is the same whatever the wavelength of light.

Why does the response increase with increase in fluence rate or irradiance? Although an increase in irradiance does not change the Pfr/P ratio it does increase the rate of interconversion of Pr and Pfr and this is significant in explaining irradiance dependent effects (see § 5.1). This phytochrome flux or 'cycling rate' may be quantified as $N\sigma_1(1-\varphi)P$ or $N\sigma_2P$ (where $(1-\varphi)P$ represents the amount of phytochrome as Pr and φP the amount as Pfr; N is the photon fluence rate; σ_1 and σ_2 are the photoconversion constants, see § 3.1). It is clearly dependent on both wavelength and irradiance. As the absolute amount of Pfr is independent of wavelength the most effective light in the high irradiance reaction is that which maintains the highest absolute rate of phytochrome flux. In seedlings Pfr and phytochrome flux operate together to produce the various photomorphogenetic responses. In contrast in seed germination the high irradiance or 'H' effect acts in the opposite direction to Pfr and can inhibit germination in both dark germinating seeds and seeds induced to germinate by a short R pulse. H can both directly antagonize the Pfr effect and also block ther germination process at a very late stage after the apparent completion of Pfr action.

	Pfr	H		
	promotes	inhibits		
⟶	⟶	⟶	⟶	germination

In seedlings which have been 'de-etiolated' by previous exposure to light the high irradiance action peak for photomorphogenesis at 720 nm disappears although R and blue light continue to be effective. It could be that the high irradiance reaction is a seedling phenomenon and does not occur in light-grown plants. However, the disappearance of the F action peak could be a consequence of the low amount of phytochrome in light-grown plants and reduced Pfr destruction.

4.12 Blue-absorbing receptor pigments

Although phytochrome absorbs in the blue region of the spectrum it has been argued that blue light acts through a different pigment. Evidence for this comes from observed qualitative differences in the effects of prolonged blue and prolonged F light. For instance, gherkin (*Cucumis sativus*) seedlings transferred from the dark to blue light show a reduced rate of hypocotyl extension after a lag of only 30 s whereas the lag period for F is 40 min. Also, lettuce seedlings at one stage of development respond to both blue and F whereas at a later stage they respond only to blue. In cucumber (*Cucumis sativus*) seedlings it is possible to show a temporal separation of the effects on stem elongation of the two photoreceptors; exposure to white light produces an immediate reduction in elongation rate mediated by the blue-absorbing receptor pigment and a delayed effect on elongation mediated by phytochrome.

In the extensively studied phototropism of grass coleoptiles it is the blue region of the spectrum which induces growth curvature towards a unilaterial source of light. Action spectra show peaks in the blue (450 and 480 nm), near ultra-violet (370 nm) and for ultra-violet (290 nm). This suggests that the response is mediated by a yellow pigment such as a carotenoid or a flavoprotein, the latter being the more likely possibility. The name *cryptochrome* has been suggested for this as yet uncharacterised receptor pigment since blue light is particularly effective in regulating morphogenesis in fungi and lower plants ('cryptogams'). For instance, blue light stimulates the transition from one-dimensional to two-dimensional growth in the development of a fern sporeling into a prothallus. Blue light is also effective in regulating chloroplast migration and stomatal movement and it has been suggested that some irradiance dependent effects on extension growth in green plants are mediated by a blue absorbing pigment. There are several examples of interactions between phytochrome and a pigment absorbing in the blue and ultra-violet regions of the spectrum. For instance, anthocyanin synthesis in *Sorghum* seedlings is dependent upon light absorption by both of the two pigments. R acting through phytochrome can modify the phototropic response of coleoptiles to a subsequent exposure to unilateral blue light. There is the possibility of very close interactions between the two pigments as suggested by energy transfer from flavin to phytochrome in complexes formed *in vitro*.

4.13   Phytochrome and plants in their natural environment

Figure 4–12 shows the spectral distribution of sunlight. It contains rather more R than F and would be expected to maintain a fairly high proportion of phytochrome in the Pfr form. Plants under natural conditions are either in the dark (low Pfr) or exposed to sunlight (high Pfr). Phytochrome is the light sensor that allows small seeds to detect that they are at or near the soil surface and that allows seedlings to detect that they have broken through the soil surface. Phytochrome also detects the beginning and end of the night in the measurement of day-length.

But what is the function of F reversibility? It should be remembered that green leaves are very effective absorbers of R light. In fact, photoreversibility can be demonstrated in light-requiring seeds by briefly exposing them to direct sunlight followed by exposure to sunlight filtered through a green leaf. Therefore, phytochrome within a leaf, particularly a leaf on a plant in dense vegetation, will be exposed to light with a relatively low R/F photon ratio. This may well be of ecological significance and perhaps give a clue to the selection pressures operating in the evolution of phytochrome as a light detector. It

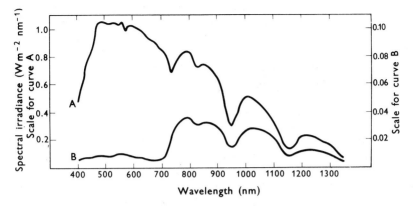

Fig. 4–12 Spectral distribution of light in the open at noon on a sunny day in July (A) compared to that of light within a woodland (B). (By courtesy of Letendre, R. J. and Frankland, B.

appears that a major function of phytochrome in nature is to detect shading and to modify growth accordingly. An example is the stem elongation response characteristic of 'shade avoiding' plants such as the weed species white goosefoot (*Chenopodium album*) (see Fig. 4–8). Seeds could also detect leaf shading through the altered light quality thus ensuring that they do not germinate under conditions where the subsequent seedlings would be unable to photosynthesize at an adequate rate for growth (see Table 3). Phytochrome is well suited to act as a quantitative detector of shade since the Pfr/P ratio changes rapidly over the range of R/F ratios found in nature. In contrast to the F enrichment of leaf shade light plants growing submerged in water are exposed to light of high R/F ratio. This may be significant in the regulation of morphogenesis in aquatic plants.

Table 3 Effect of leaf shading on seed germination in *Plantago major*. Percentage germination after one week of seeds sown on the soil surface under mustard plants (densities ranging from 3 to 45 plants dm^{-2}), grown in day-light in a glasshouse at 25°C. The degree of shading indicated by leaf area index (ratio of total leaf area to soil area). Corresponding values given for red/far-red (R/F) photon ratio of light at soil surface and for estimated φ. (Data from Frankland, B. and Poo, W. K. (1980). In: *Photorecetors and Plant Development*, p. 357. Ed. J. De Greef, University Press, Antwerp.)

Leaf area index	R/F ratio	φ	Percentage germination
0	1.18	0.59	95
1.5	0.62	0.51	89
3.9	0.22	0.32	26
4.5	0.14	0.23	14
7.2	0.10	0.19	5

5 Mode of Action of Phytochrome

5.1 Analysis of phytochrome action

Pfr is regarded as the physiologically active form of phytochrome (see § 4.4). Conversion of Pr to Pfr by light will produce a particular response depending on the localization of the phytochrome and the state of differentiation of the responding cell or cells.

Pfr action has been studied in two main experimental situations. Firstly, conversion of Pr to Pfr by a single short pulse of red light (R), the induced response being followed in the subsequent dark period. Secondly, by continuous irradiation with far-red light (F) maintaining a low but constant (steady state) Pfr/P ratio. The first method allows the time course of escape from F reversion to be followed. This gives an indication of the time course of Pfr action. Application of metabolic inhibitors before and after irradiation can be used to give some indication of the prerequisites for Pfr action and the nature of Pfr action. However, it is often difficult to separate effects on Pfr action from effects on later processes leading up to the response.

There are several steps between the initial action of Pfr and the final response. Very little is known about this sequence of events.

Attention has been focused on phytochrome controlled biochemical changes since here there is a greater chance of tracing back the sequence of biochemical steps to the point of initial Pfr action. R–F reversibility has been observed in relation to the synthesis of pigments such as chlorophyll, carotenoids and flavonoids (e.g. anthocyanins). There is also phytochrome control of the breakdown of carbohydrates and other food reserves in seedlings. For instance, starch stored in the leaves of maize seedlings is mobilized more rapidly in R irradiated seedlings as compared to seedlings maintained continuously in the dark.

The fact that phytochrome is a protein led to the idea that Pfr was the active form of an enzyme. Light induced changes in the chromophore lead to changes in the conformation of the protein which could increase the accessibility of certain active groups (e.g. SH groups) which then allows binding with the substrate. However, there is no indication of the nature of the substrate nor is there any convincing experimental evidence that phytochrome is an enzyme. Nevertheless, the general idea that conversion of Pr to Pfr involves a

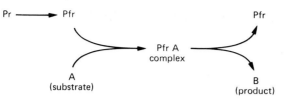

conformational change in the protein followed by binding to some receptor molecule or 'reaction partner' (X) has been retained. For instance, Song has suggested that movement of the chromophore exposes a hydrophobic binding site on the protein (see Fig. 3–4). The development in a tissue of 'competence' to respond to Pfr is often explained in terms of an increase in the amount or receptivity of X.

In the case of the high irradiance reaction, response is not only dependent on Pfr, but also on the rate of interconversion of Pr and Pfr (see § 4.11). Hartmann suggested that there might be an excited species of Pfr (Pfr*) which was more active than Pfr in the ground state; under continuous light the proportion of phytochrome as Pfr* would increase with increase in irradiance. It is also possible that Pfr* is one of the intermediates described in section 3.1. However, there is no evidence for either of these possibilities.

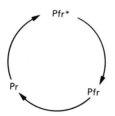

Schäfer (1975) attempted to explain the differences between the high irradiance reaction and the low energy, inductive reaction in terms of changes in the PfrX complex. PfrX' is the state present in the dark following a brief irradiation whereas the high irradiance reaction could be mediated by the state PfrX. As the reaction PfrX → PfrX' is slower than the reaction Pfr+X → PfrX, it is the latter state which will tend to accumulate under continuous, high irradiance. Both these dark (d) reactions are slower than the photoreactions (indicated below as hv). Schäfer's model is a mathematical one and in its complete form takes account of both Pr synthesis and Pfr destruction; it can be used to explain why the high irradiance peak of action is in the F region of the spectrum.

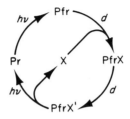

The possibility that the actual conversion of Pr to Pfr could drive some reaction has been considered for a long time. Johnson and Tasker in 1979 suggested that under high irradiance conditions the continuous interconversion of Pr to Pfr could be coupled to the movement of some metabolite (Y) across a membrane. Response is dependent upon both Pfr and Y.

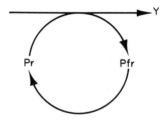

5.2   Phytochrome and gene expression

It is generally accepted that most living cells of a particular plant contain all the genetic information (in the form of DNA, deoxyribonucleic acid) characteristic of that plant. Differences amongst cells must arise from differential gene activity, genes being 'turned off' and 'turned on' during development. Many of the responses controlled by phytochrome involve changes in the direction of differentiation and hence changes in the pattern of gene activity. This led Mohr in 1966 to suggest that phytochrome might act by controlling gene activity. He proposed that 'primary' differentiation of a cell produced a certain pattern of gene activity with some of the inactive genes having the potential for being activated by Pfr and some of the active genes being capable of being repressed by Pfr. The changes resulting from Pfr action he described as 'secondary' differentiation.

The sequence of amino acids in a protein is coded for by the sequence of nucleotide bases in the DNA, the flow of information being summarized as follows:

TRANSCRIPTION   TRANSLATION

DNA (gene) ───────────► messenger RNA ───────────► protein

    nucleus   cytoplasm
  (chromosomes)   (ribosomes)

Metabolic inhibitors have been used to explore the point of action of Pfr
although the results of such experiments have to be interpreted with caution.
For instance, actinomycin-D, an inhibitor of transcription (i.e. DNA-
dependent RNA synthesis), will inhibit certain phytochrome controlled
responses. This may only indicate that Pfr action or a later process in the
response is dependent on RNA synthesis rather than that Pfr acts by
stimulating RNA synthesis.

Increased ribosomal RNA synthesis has sometimes been observed in
association with phytochrome controlled growth responses although this may
be a consequence of increased growth rather than a direct result of Pfr action.
The appearance of polyribosomes in dark-grown leaves exposed to light can be
taken as suggesting messenger RNA synthesis although, again, there is no
strong evidence that this is a very direct result of Pfr action.

Some phytochrome controlled responses are relatively insensitive to RNA
synthesis inhibitors but can be blocked by inhibitors of protein synthesis such as
puromycin or cycloheximide. This could suggest that phytochrome is acting at
the level of translation (i.e. in mRNA guided synthesis of proteins on the
ribosomes) rather than at the level of transcription.

5.3   Phytochrome and enzyme synthesis

Whatever the mode of action of Pfr there is little doubt that it often leads to
changes in the pattern of enzymes present. For instance, seedling photomorphogenesis is associated with the appearance of enzymes necessary for
photosynthesis. NADP-dependent glyceraldehyde-3-phosphate dehydro-
genase, an enzyme associated with leaf chloroplasts, was one of the first
enzymes in which changes in activity were shown to be R–F reversible.

An enzyme which has been extensively studied is phenylalanine ammonia
lyase. This enzyme catalyses the conversion of the amino acid phenylalanine to
cinnamic acid and thus redirects metabolism away from protein synthesis and
towards synthesis of various phenolic compounds such as the red anthocyanin

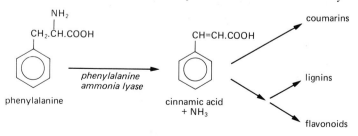

pigments and other flavonoids. Other substances eventually formed by this pathway include lignin, a constituent of secondary cell walls, and coumarin (responsible for the smell of new mown hay). The enzyme is present in very low concentrations in mustard seedlings grown in the dark but can be greatly increased by exposure to light. The time course of changes in enzyme activity on transfer from dark to F light is shown in Fig. 5–1. There is a lag phase of about one h and then a rise in enzyme activity, followed by a fall in activity after about 20 h. Such kinetics can be interpreted in terms of the following sequence of events: (*i*) induction of enzyme synthesis, (*ii*) inactivation of enzyme, (*iii*) repression of enzyme synthesis. Inactivation and repression are initiated by the

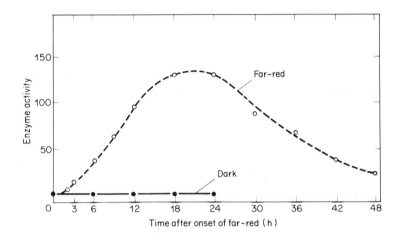

Fig. 5–1 Kinetics of appearance of the enzyme phenylalanine ammonia lyase in cotyledons of mustard seedlings exposed to continuous far-red light. Enzyme activity expressed as cinnamic acid formed (pmol min^{-1} per pair of cotyledons). (Redrawn from Dittes, L., Rissland, I. and Mohr, H. (1971). *Naturforsch.*, **26b**, 1175.)

build-up of end products of enzyme action such as cinnamic acid and *p*-courmaric acid.

The increase in enzyme activity can be blocked by protein synthesis inhibitors but this is not rigorous proof that there is an actual increase in the number of enzyme molecules. There is always doubts as to the specificity of action of a given inhibitor and, in any case, an inhibitory effect only indicates that protein synthesis is a pre-requisite for the process. Density labelling experiments do provide some evidence that *de novo* enzyme synthesis is taking place. Such experiments involve growing seedlings in heavy water (D_2O, deuterium oxide), extracting the enzyme and determining its density by appropriate centrifugation techniques. During hydrolysis of storage protein, deuterium is incorporated into the amino acids formed. These 'heavy' amino acids will become incorporated into newly synthesized protein and thus increase its density relative to protein synthesized in seedlings grown in ordinary water. Even the interpretation of this type of experiment has been criticized by some scientists who claim there is still no convincing proof that Pfr action leads to sythesis of the phenylalanine ammonia lyase enzyme. They suggest the effect of Pfr could be on activation of previously synthesized enzyme molecules. However, there is agreement that Pfr action results in the synthesis of some enzymes, e.g. ascorbic acid oxidase. In most cases Pfr simply alters the rate of synthesis of enzymes already present in seedlings grown in the dark. This is difficult to explain on the basis of a simple model of induction of enzyme synthesis.

Some enzymes, such as lipoxygenase, are formed in the dark in mustard seedlings but are completely inhibited by Pfr. Other enzymes such as catalase and isocitrate lyase appear to be unaffected by light.

5.4 Phytochrome and membrane related phenomena

Although changes in gene activity are an eventual consequence of Pfr action there is no evidence that this is the primary mode of action of phytochrome. Some photoresponses are so rapid that it is difficult to believe that gene action and protein synthesis are involved. Such a rapid response is the phytochrome controlled dark closure or folding of the leaflets of the legume plants *Mimosa* and *Samanea*. The movement involves differential changes in turgor in the cells of the pulvinus at the base of each leaflet; there is a decrease in turgor in adaxial ('extensor') cells and an increase in turgor in abaxial ('flexor') cells. These changes in hydrostatic pressure result from the osmotic water movement which follows the movement of potassium, chloride and other ions out of extensor cells and into flexor cells. In several other systems, e.g. hypocotyl sections of mung bean (*Phaseolus aureus*), ion fluxes have been shown to be modulated by phytochrome. The rapidity of these responses points to changes in membrane permeability or other membrane properties as early consequences of Pfr action.

Further evidence of membrane changes following Pfr action came from Tanada's discovery that excised barley (*Hordeum vulgare*) and mung bean root tips exposed to R would stick to a negatively charged glass surface. This peculiar phenomenon of light induced adhesion was found to be R–F reversible. It was suggested that the apical part of the root segment became electro-positive relative to the basal part in response to the formation of Pfr. Measurements of the potential difference between apex and base confirmed this. The changes in electrical potential were only about 1 mV but developed within 30 s of the light treatment. Rapid phytochrome controlled changes in electric potential have also been measured in the coleoptiles of oat seedlings. These electrical changes are consistent with a phytochrome induced efflux of ions. Jaffe's observation of R induced changes in acetylcholine levels in plant tissues suggested similarities between Pfr action and the generation of an action potential in the nerve fibres of animals. However, there is no evidence for the involvement of acetylcholine in other phytochrome controlled responses.

Potassium fluxes in leaf pulvini are preceded by transmembrane potential changes suggesting phytochrome control of the transport of another ion (e.g. a proton-sucrose co-transport system). An important aspect of these rapid, phytochrome controlled membrane phenomena is that the *response* (the change in electric potential) is reversible by F (Fig. 5–2). This is evidence that these effects are close to the primary site of action of phytochrome.

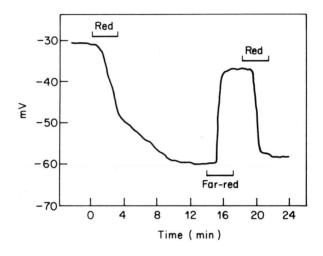

Fig. 5–2   Phytochrome controlled changes in the transmembrane electric potential of flexor cells in a leaf pulvinus of *Samanea*. Pfr causes rapid hyperpolarisation (more negative) whereas conversion of Pfr to Pr is followed by rapid depolarization. (Redrawn from Racusen, R. and Satter, R. L. (1975). *Nature*, **255**, 407.)

5.5   Intracellular localization of phytochrome

Elegant experiments carried out by Haupt between 1960 and 1970 on the photocontrol of chloroplast movement (Fig. 5–3) in the alga *Mougeotia* have established that phytochrome is located not in the chloroplast but in or near the plasma membrane. Using microbeams and polarized light it was shown that Pr must have its axis of maximum absorption in the plane of the cell surface whereas Pfr has its axis at right angles to the cell surface. There is *dichroic* orientation of the phytochrome molecules. This means that unilateral R will tend to transform Pr to Pfr more readily at the front and back of the cell compared to the sides. Assuming that the flat chloroplast moves away from regions of the cytoplasm with high Pfr levels then an explanation is provided for the orientation of the chloroplast at right angles to the incident light. This is illustrated diagrammatically in Fig. 5–4.

Fern sporelings will show growth curvatures related to the plane of vibration of the electrical vector of polarized light. Growth takes place at the tip of the apical cell and the response to polarized light can be explained in terms of phytochrome molecules orientated in the peripheral cytoplasm. Such

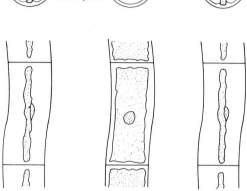

Fig. 5–3 Phytochrome control of chloroplast orientation in cells of the alga *Mougeotia*. Cells shown in cross-section and surface view. R, orientation of chloroplast 30 min after 1 min irradiation with red light. R–F, orientation of chloroplast 30 min after irradiation with 1 min red light immediately followed by 1 min far-red light. (Redrawn from Haupt, W. (1970). *Physiol, veg.*, **8**, 551, Editions Gauthier–Villars, Paris.)

experiments do not rule out the possibility of phytochrome being located in other parts of the cell. For instance, R–F reversible changes have been observed in isolated organelles such as plastids (see § 4.5).

Attempts have been made to locate phytochrome within the cell by immuno-cytochemical methods (see § 2.4). Results obtained with the latter technique suggest that phytochrome is present in the cytoplasm as well as being associated with cell organelles (see § 3.3). Following photoconversion to the Pfr form phytochrome appears to become concentrated or 'sequestered' at a few discrete sites within the cell (see Fig. 2–9). The physiological significance and general relevance of this phenomenon is not clear.

Using spectrophotometric techniques phytochrome has been detected in association with cell organelles, such as plastids and mitochondria, isolated by tissue homogenization and differential centrifugation. During normal methods of phytochrome extraction a small proportion of the total phytochrome does appear in the pellet following centrifugation. Work by Marmé and others has shown that irradiation of the tissue with R before homogenization increases the proportion of phytochrome which is 'pelletable'. Their work suggests that phytochrome in the Pfr form binds readily to membrane fragments. These results may be an artefact associated with cell homogenization but, on the other hand, they may give a clue to the site of

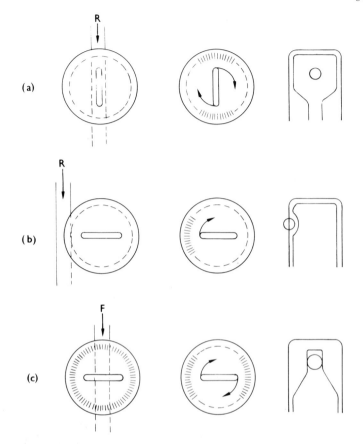

Fig. 5–4 Diagrammatic representation of three experiments involving irradiation of *Mougeotia* cells with red (R) or far-red (F) microbeams. In (**a**) and (**b**) cells previously in dark; in (**c**) cells previously in light. *Left:* cross-sections showing starting condition and position of microbeam. *Centre:* cross-sections showing conditions after phytochrome photoconversion, curved arrows show direction of movement of chloroplast. *Right:* surface view with position of microbeam and response of chloroplast. Tangentially oriented dashes indicate Pr; radial dashes indicate Pfr. Note how the chloroplast moves away from Pfr. (Redrawn from Haupt, W. (1970). *Physiol, veg.*, **8**, 551, Editions Gauthier–Villars, Paris.)

action of Pfr. X, the Pfr reaction partner, may be a membrane component. It is possible that Pr as well as Pfr is associated with membranes *in vivo* but the former is bound less tenaciously so that it becomes detached during homogenization.

5.6   Phytochrome action in membranes

The association between phytochrome and a membrane provides a structural basis for the orientation of phytochrome molecules and also for possible co-operative interaction between Pfr molecules. Light induced changes in the phytochrome chromophore leads to changes in the conformation of the phytochrome protein. This in turn could lead to changes in membrane conformation and hence to changes in membrane function. It has been suggested that the association of Pfr with a membrane makes the latter more permeable, allowing the passive diffusion of some essential ion or other metabolite along a concentration or electrochemical gradient. It has also been suggested that phytochrome 'cycling' could be coupled to the active 'pumping' of some molecule across a membrane. These two ideas can be combined to produce a speculative model to explain how Pfr and phytochrome flux (H) could act synergistically in seedling photomorphogenesis but antagonistically in seed germination (Fig. 5–5).

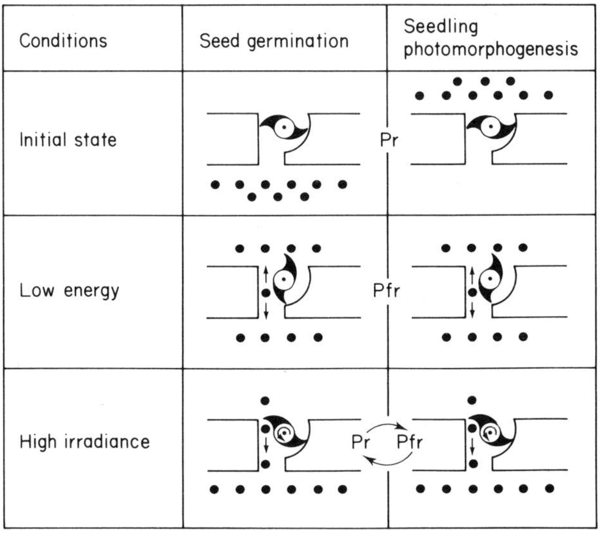

Fig. 5–5 Speculative model to explain interaction of Pfr and phytochrome flux in seedling morphogenesis and seed germination. Formation of Pfr is shown as opening a 'gate' in the membrane allowing diffusion of some ion or metabolite from one side to the other. Continuous cycling of Pr and Pfr is shown as 'pumping' the same ion or metabolite across the membrane. In seed germination the 'pump' operates in the opposite direction to the concentration or electrochemical gradient.

The movement of the chloroplast in a *Mougeotia* cell is brought about by the contraction of actomyosin-like filaments which connect the chloroplast to the plasmamembrane. The contractile activity of the filaments is regulated by calcium (Ca^{2+}) ions through a Ca-dependent ATPase. Phytochrome could control the spatial distribution of Ca^{2+} ions through changes in membrane properties, the source of the Ca^{2+} being either the external medium or organelles such as mitochondria (see Fig. 5–6). Ca-dependent enzymes, such as ATPase and NAD kinase, are activated by the regulatory protein calmodulin; the latter reversibly binds Ca^{2+} and is activated when the Ca^{2+} ion concentration rises about 10^{-6}M.

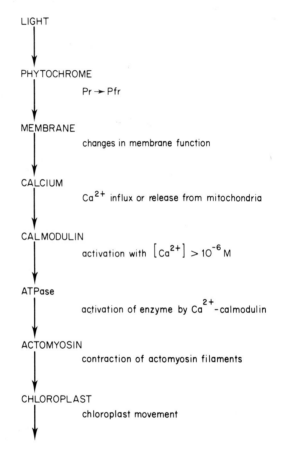

LIGHT

↓

PHYTOCHROME

    Pr → Pfr

↓

MEMBRANE

    changes in membrane function

↓

CALCIUM

    Ca^{2+} influx or release from mitochondria

↓

CALMODULIN

    activation with $[Ca^{2+}] > 10^{-6}$ M

↓

ATPase

    activation of enzyme by Ca^{2+}-calmodulin

↓

ACTOMYOSIN

    contraction of actomyosin filaments

↓

CHLOROPLAST

    chloroplast movement

↓

Fig. 5–6 Phytochrome control of chloroplast orientation in *Mougeotia*: probable sequence of events.

It should be stressed that permeability change is only one possible consequence of change in membrane function. For instance, there could be changes in the activity of membrane bound enzymes. Release of 'messenger substances' must also be a possibility since the biochemical response may be remote from the site of Pfr action, say in the nucleus of the same cell or in the nucleus or cytoplasm of another cell. Calcium may be regarded as such a messenger. Plant hormones will be involved in signal transmission over longer distances. In this context the Pfr induced rapid release of gibberellin from etioplasts is of some interest (see § 4.5).

The variety of phytochrome-controlled responses could arise from a variety of processes at the site of phytochrome action or conversely there could be a single primary process acting in different cellular environments. There could be a variety of membrane associated Pfr reaction partners (X_1, X_2, X_3, etc.) or a variety of 'second messengers' (Y_1, Y_2, Y_3, etc.) released from or transported across a membrane. The speculative model in Fig. 5–5 assumes that both Pfr induced responses and phytochrome cycling dependent responses arise from the same primary mode of action; the variety of response could arise from the states of primary differentiation of the cells concerned.

6 Some Practical Exercises

6.1 Construction of simple light sources

These light sources should be used in a dark room, preferably maintained at 25°C by means of a fan heater and thermostat.

Red light

Material to be irradiated is placed in a cardboard box with a lid consisting of one layer of No. 14 Ruby and one layer of No. 1 Yellow Cinemoid[1] filter placed beneath two 40 watt fluorescent tubes. Phytochrome photoconversion will be complete after a 5 min exposure to this source.

Far-red light

Material to be irradiated is placed in a cardboard box with a lid consisting of one layer of No. 5a Deep Orange and one layer of No. 20 Deep Blue (Primary) Cinemoid filter. The box is placed beneath four 60 watt incandescent lamps and separated from them by a 10 cm depth of water in a glass or clear plastic container. Phytochrome photoconversion will be complete after a 5 min exposure to this source.

Green safe-light

Fluorescent tube wrapped with at least 3 layers of No. 39 Primary Green Cinemoid filter.

White light

In studies of the 'high irradiance' effects of prolonged white light the most convenient light source is a bank of incandescent lamps. The plant material under study should be separated from the lights by a heat filter of water and should also be cooled by moving air from a fan. A second fan is necessary to remove hot air from around the lamps. For temperature control it is also necessary to have positive cooling from a refrigeration system.

---

[1] Cinemoid filter obtainable from Rank Strand Electric Ltd., P.O. Box 51, Great West Road, Brentford, Middlesex, U.K.
[2] Grand Rapids lettuce seeds obtainable from Philip Harris Biological Ltd., Oldmixon, Weston-super-Mare, Avon BS24 9BJ, U.K.

6.2 Phytochrome control of seed germination

Sow about 50 seeds of lettuce[2] (*Lactuca sativa*) of the variety Grand Rapids on 2 layers of filter paper moistened with 2 cm³ of water in a 5 cm petri dish. Immediately place the dishes in a cardboard box wrapped in black polythene and maintain at 25°C in an incubator. Use 2 dishes for each of the following treatments: (*i*) complete darkness, (*ii*) 5 min red light (R), (*iii*) 5 min R followed immediately by 5 min far-red (F) light. Irradiation treatments should be given 2 h after sowing in the dark with seeds being returned to darkness after treatment. Manipulations must be carried out in darkness or under a green safe-light. After 24 h count the number of germinated and ungerminated seeds and express the results as percentage germination.

A given batch of lettuce seeds may be unsuitable for demonstrating the effects of light because percentage germination in the dark is high. Often a better light response can be obtained by working at a temperature higher than 25°C. Alternatively seeds of wild species[1] may be collected during late summer or autumn. Common weed species which are known to have a light requirement for germination include great plantain (*Plantago major*), white goosefoot (*Chenopodium album*) and broad leaved dock (*Rumex obtusifolius*). Other examples include foxglove (*Digitalis purpurea*) and self-heal (*Prunella vulgaris*).

Freshly harvested seeds usually need to be dried and stored for a few weeks before they develop their ability to respond to light. Light effects on germination are strongly conditioned by temperature in a way that varies from species to species. Therefore, the temperature for maximum differences in percentage germination between dark and light treatments should be determined by prior experimentation. Note that there will also be variation from species to species in the time after sowing when seeds are most responsive to light and in the time to germination. For instance, *Plantago major* seeds at 25°C are most responsive to a single pulse of light 24 h after sowing and take 5 days to germinate. *Plantago* seeds often require repeated pulses of light (e.g. 5 min R every day for 3 days) to induce maximum germination.

A number of cultivated flower species[2] are useful for investigating the photoinhibition of germination by white light. These include *Amaranthus caudatus* (love-lies-bleeding), *Nemophila insignis* (baby-blue-eyes), *Nigella damascena* (love-in-a-mist) and *Phacelia tanacetifolia*. Compare germination in the dark with that under continuous white incandescent light. Seed dishes in the light should be placed on a layer of wet blotting paper inside a transparent polythene bag. Investigate the effect of low irradiance light by convering some of the dishes in the light with 16 layers of muslin cloth (this reduces light to 10% of the original value). Also investigate the effects of such light conditions on the germination of a light-requiring species.

[1] Seeds of British wild plants are also obtainable from Emorsgate seeds, Emorsgate, Terrington St. Clement, King's Lynn, Norfolk PE34 4NY, U.K.

[2] Seeds of flower species obtainable from Thompson and Morgan (Ipswich) Ltd., London Road, Ipswich IP2 0BA, U.K.

6.3   Phytochrome control of seedling growth

Investigate the growth and development of seedlings in darkness and in continuous white light over a 2 week time period. Use species with large seeds, and hence large seedlings, and compare seedlings of three contrasting types. Soak seeds for 4 h in water in the dark and then sow in a seed tray or plant pot in moist vermiculite or soil. Measure epicotyl length and leaf area (or leaf fresh weight) in seedlings of pea (*Pisum sativum*) or broad bean (*Vicia faba*). Measure hypocotyl length and cotyledon area in seedlings of sunflower (*Helianthus annus*) or French bean (*Phaseolus vulgaris*) or cucumber (*Cucumis sativus*) or mustard (*Sinapis alba*). Measure first internode length, coleoptile length, and length and 'apparent' width of first true leaf in seedlings of maize (*Zea mays*) or oat (*Avena sativa*).

Investigate phytochrome control by comparing seedlings grown in complete darkness with seedlings irradiated each day with either 5 min R or 5 min R followed by 5 min F. Begin irradiation treatments after seeds have germinated and seedlings are in the early stages of growth. Select 10 seedlings of similar size for each treatment. Measure growth after a further 4 days. Carry out all manipulations under a green safe-light.

6.4   Phytochrome control of chlorophyll synthesis

Plant grown in darkness are etiolated and lack chlorophyll. Light is necessary for the direct photochemical conversion of protochlorophyllide into chlorophyllide and also for regulating an earlier step in the pathway of chlorophyll biosynthesis.

light   *light*
(phytochrome)
$\longrightarrow \longrightarrow \longrightarrow$ protochlorophyllide $\longrightarrow$ chlorophyllide $\longrightarrow$ chlorophyll

On transfer of dark-grown seedlings to white light there is a lag phase of about 5 h before the main phase of chlorophyll synthesis. A previous brief exposure to light will eliminate this lag phase.

Investigate the time course of appearance of chlorophyll in leaves of 7 day old dark-grown barley (*Hordeum vulgare*) seedlings transferred to white light. Give the barley seedlings the following pre-treatments: (*i*) 6 h dark, (*ii*) 5 min R followed by 6 h dark, (*iii*) 5 min R followed by 5 min F and then 6 h dark. After 0, 60, 120 and 180 min extract and measure chlorophyll from duplicate samples of leaves.

For each sample take 2 cm apical portions from 20 primary leaves. Weigh the sample after wrapping in a pre-weighed piece of aluminium foil. Thoroughly homogenize the leaf material in a pestle and mortar with 5 cm^3 of 80% acetone in water (v/v). Clarify the resulting homogenate by low speed centrifugation in a bench centrifuge. Decant off the supernatant and make up to a final volume of 10 cm^3. Pour some of the extract into a 1 cm pathlength *glass* cuvette and measure the absorbance at 663 nm (the red absorption peak of chlorophyll a) using a spectrophotometer (or use a colorimeter with a red filter). Zero the instrument with a reference cuvette containing only 80% acetone. Calculate the chlorophyll concentration in the extract in μmol dm^{-3} assuming that the molar extinction coefficient (see § 1.3) for total chlorophyll (a + b) at 663 nm in 80% acetone is 6×10^{-4} μmol^{-1} dm^{-3} cm^{-1} and then calculate the amount of chlorophyll in the leaf material in μmol per g fresh weight.

Further Reading

Studies in Biology

BRADY, J. (1974). *Biological Clocks.* No. 104 Edward Arnold, London.
WHATLEY, J. M. and WHATLEY, F. R. (1980). *Light and Plant Life.* No. 124 Edward Arnold, London.

Books

HAUPT, W. and FEINLEIB, M. E. (1979). (Eds.) *Physiology of Movements.* Encyclopaedia of Plant Physiology, New Series, Springer-Verlag, Berlin, Heidelberg and London.
MITRAKOS, K. and SHROPSHIRE Jr., W. (1972). (Eds.) *Phytochrome.* Academic Press, London and New York.
MOHR, H. (1972). *Lectures on photomorphogenesis.* Springer-Verlag, Berlin, Heidelberg and London.
SHROPSHIRE Jr., W. and MOHR, H. (in press) (Eds.) *Photomorphogenesis.* Encyclopaedia of Plant Physiology, New Series. Springer-Verlag, Berlin, Heidelberg and London.
SMITH, H. (1975). *Phytochrome and Photomorphogenesis.* McGraw-Hill Book Co., London and New York.
SMITH, H. (in press) (Ed.) *Techniques in Photomorphogenesis.* Academic Press, London and New York.
SMITH, H. (1981). (Ed.) *Plants and the Daylight Spectrum.* Academic Press, London and New York.
SMITH, K. C. (1977). *The Science of Photobiology.* Plenum Press, New York.
VINCE-PRUE, D. (1975). *Photoperiodism in Plants.* McGraw-Hill Book Co., London and New York.
VINCE-PRUE, D. and COSENS, D. (in press), (Eds.) *The Biology of Photoreceptors* S.E.B. Symposium No. 36, University Press, Cambridge.

Review articles

KENDRICK, R. E. and SMITH, H. (1976). The assay of isolation of phytochrome. In *Chemistry and Biochemistry of Plant Pigments.* Volume 2, Ed. T. W. GOODWIN. 2nd Edition, p. 334. Academic Press, London and New York.
KENDRICK, R. E. and SPRUIT, C. J. P. (1977). Phototransformations of phytochrome. *Photochem Photobiol.*, **26**, 201.
PRATT, L. H. (1978). The molecular properties of phytochrome. *Photochem. Photobiol.*, **27**, 81.
PRATT, L. H. (1979). Phytochrome: function and properties. In *Photochemical and Photobiological Reviews*, Vol. 4. Ed. K. C. SMITH, p. 59, Plenum Press, New York.
PRATT, L. H. (1982). Phytochrome: The protein moiety. *Annual Review of Plant Physiol.*, **33**, 557.
SMITH, H. (1982). Light quality, photoreception and plant strategy. *Annual Review of Plant Physiol.*, **33**, 481.

Index